Parents, Let's Talk Money!

If you're not talking to your Teen about it - who is?

By Lesley Thomas

Published in 2025 by Discover Your Bounce Publishing
www.discoveryourbouncepublishing.com
Copyright © Discover Your Bounce Publishing
All rights reserved.
Printed in the United States of America & the UK. No part of this book may be used, replicated or reproduced, stored in a retrieval system, or transmitted in any form or by any means, electronic, mechanical, photocopying, recording, or otherwise, without the written permission of the author(s). Quotations of no more than 25 words are permitted, but only if used solely for the purposes of critical articles or reviews.

ISBN: 978-1-914428-42-5

Although the author and publisher have made every effort to ensure that the information in this book is correct at the time of going to print, the author and publisher do not assume and therefore disclaim liability to any party. The author and the publisher will not be held responsible for any loss or damage save for that caused by their negligence.

Although the author and the publisher have made every reasonable attempt to achieve accuracy in the content of this book, they assume no responsibility for errors or omissions.

Page design and typesetting by Discover Your Bounce Publishing

CONTENTS

Dedication	i
Acknowledgements	ii
Foreword	iv
Introduction	ix
Chapter 1 – Starting the Money Conversation	1
Chapter 2 – The Importance of Money Conversation	15
Chapter 3 – Building Money Confidence – For you and Your Teen	34
Chapter 4 – Understanding Basic Money Concepts Together	48
Chapter 5 – Setting Financial Goals	56
Chapter 6 – The Power of Budgeting (Soft Landing Fund)	66
Chapter 7 – Navigating Digital Money and Online Spending	92
Chapter 8 – Understanding Credit and Avoiding Debt	113
Chapter 9 – How to Have Difficult Conversation About Money	135
Chapter 10 – Helping Your Teen Stay Safe Online	159
Chapter 11 – Growing Wealth Together as a Family	177
Chapter 12 – Conversations with Your Future Self	209
Additional Resources	245
About the Author	250

DEDICATION

To 'My Boys', who taught me all that matters. And to my parents, who encouraged me to dream big.

ACKNOWLEDGEMENTS

Writing this book has been both a personal and professional journey, one shaped by the experiences I've had, the clients I've worked with and the deeply held belief that when parents change their relationship with money, they change everything for the next generation. To every parent who has ever sat with the discomfort of a difficult money conversation, thank you. Your courage is the spark that inspired this book.

To my clients, the wildly ambitious women who chose to look inward, challenge their money stories, and do the work, your transformation has fuelled my passion, sharpened my insight and reaffirmed that money confidence is always possible.

To the incredible educators and school leaders I've had the privilege to collaborate with, your commitment to financial education and wellbeing in schools is paving the way for real, lasting change.

To my publishers, Nicky and Sharon at Discover your Bounce, thank you for believing in this message and guiding it into the world with care, professionalism and thoughtfulness.

To Penny Power OBE, thank you for lending your

voice to this work. Your foreword added warmth, wisdom, and weight to the message I'm sharing. I'm deeply honoured.

To my two sons, Adam and Sam, thank you for being my 'why.' You are the reason I do this work and your questions, growth and challenges have made me a better mother and mentor.

To Steve, thank you for believing in me, especially in the moments I needed it most. Your support has been a constant I'm deeply grateful for.

To my team, mentors and those behind the scenes, your contributions, ideas, and encouragement have helped bring this book into the world. I'm thankful for your belief in this mission.

And finally, to every reader, thank you for picking up this book. May it help you have the conversations that matter, build confidence that lasts, and lead your family into a financially empowered future.

Where Mindset goes, Money Grows®.

Lesley

Foreword

By Penny Power OBE

When Lesley asked me to write the foreword to this book, I felt an immediate "yes" rise in my energy. I believe in the mission of this book, and I believe in the transformational power of the conversations it will spark between parents and their teens.

We can all reflect on our own experience with money, the relationship we have with it, how it may have limited us, or perhaps the positive way it has enabled us. Working with entrepreneurs, start-ups and even within Further Education Collages since 1998, I have been able to almost predict the outcomes of ambitions being met, by the level in which people respect and honour financial disciplines, and those that fear and avoid the topic.

For this reason, I was motivated to build financial discipline and understanding into our three children very early on. Now seeing them as thriving entrepreneurial adults, I am believed I did a good job at this. However, I also passed onto them some of my limiting beliefs. Many fears from my own experience; from childhood family beliefs, plus my own challenging journey with money. This book ensures we understand ourselves, before we begin to create the beliefs that will help our own children thrive peacefully.

Lesley and I first connected within a community where business owners come together not just to grow their businesses, but to grow as people. From the moment Lesley joined, she brought a quiet strength and a grounded passion that drew people in. Her message was a critical topic, one that we all resonated with as entrepreneurs and as parents. The message that money isn't just about spreadsheets and savings. It's about mindset, self-worth, and the stories we carry, often in silence, from generation to generation.

As I've got to know Lesley, I've come to admire the way she weaves emotional intelligence with practical guidance. She has a gift for meeting people exactly where they are, never judging, only supporting. And that's exactly what this book does too.

"Parents: Let's Talk Money!" is not your typical money

manual. It's a gentle but powerful call to action. A nudge to break the silence. A warm, encouraging guide for parents who want to do things differently, even if they never learned how to do it right themselves. And let's face it, most of us didn't, there are generations of people that never found peace due to their lack of understanding of finance and the money that they held, many for just a short time.

For many of us growing up, money wasn't a conversation. It was a source of tension. Or confusion. Or fear. We inherited unspoken rules and invisible scripts, phrases like "money doesn't grow on trees," or "we can't afford that". It's no wonder so many adults today carry guilt, shame, or anxiety around their finances.

Lesley understands this deeply, not just in theory, but from lived experience. She knows what it feels like to want to support your child with everything you have. She knows that our relationship with money is rarely about money. It's about identity. Safety. Permission and possibility.

And what makes this book so special is that it doesn't preach. It is your friend. Lesley has created a resource that walks *with* you, beside you. She invites you into reflection. Into honesty, to step into courage. She opens the door to conversations that can change not only your teen's financial future, but yours too.

Reading this book, I found myself nodding, underlining, and pausing often. Not just because of the wisdom Lesley shares, but because of the compassion behind every word. You feel held as you read it. You feel seen and her navigation of this subject is relatable.

There's something extraordinary about a book that teaches and heals at the same time.

As parents, we are, often unwittingly, the authors of our children's money story. What Lesley offers here is the chance to write a new chapter. One where honesty replaces fear. One where learning becomes a shared experience. One where a family's financial legacy is built not on silence or struggle, but on understanding, empowerment, and open-hearted conversation.

This book gives you the tools. But more importantly, it

gives you permission to show up imperfectly, to learn out loud, and to lead with love.

To the parent reading this now, perhaps with a little apprehension or self-doubt: you are not alone. And you don't have to be perfect to start. In fact, your willingness to grow alongside your teen may be the most powerful teaching of all.

And to the teen who may pick this up one day, know that this book exists because someone believes in your potential to create a life of financial confidence, freedom, and choice.

Lesley has written the book we all wish had been handed to us when we were young. The good news is, it's here now for you, your family, and the generations that follow.

So, take a breath. Turn the page. The conversation starts now. With warmth, respect, gratitude, and good fortune.

Penny Power OBE

Introduction

Why talking about money matters. Money: it's something we all use, think about and deal with every day, but how often do we *really* talk about it? If you're a teen reading this, the chances are you've heard adults talking loosely about money, but has someone, particularly your parents, sat you down to really explain it? And if you are a parent, be really honest, when was the last time you had an open conversation with your Teen about money and what it really means?

The truth is money talks. Money has a big influence on our lives, whether we proactively want it to or not. And this extends, whether or not you realise it, to your relationship with money, which shapes so many aspects of your life. It directly impacts the choice you make, the opportunities you are able to access, the decisions you take and most importantly, how confident you feel about your future. Yet, in many families, money is still a taboo topic. We would rather talk about sex than money. As a society we have a quiet understanding, or a subconscious agreement, that money is somehow uncomfortable, too personal or even inappropriate. But I am here to challenge that belief, starting now.

So why start having the money conversation now?
For your Teen, the years immediately ahead are pivotal. They might be preparing to leave school, thinking about higher education, or starting an apprenticeship or job. They may even be managing their own money for the first time; and as a parent, it is your job to ensure they feel confident in the decisions they need to make, because they have been provided with the information they need to make the right decision. Whether your Teen is saving for driving lessons, their first car, considering a gap year, or simply trying to manage the money they are earning from a part-time job, they will have questions, they will need information, as there will be decisions they need to make, that require solid financial understanding and confidence in taking the right action.

I know that for parents, it can feel scary to guide your Teen through this period in both of your lives, especially when no one talked to you about money when you were their age. Don't beat yourself up.

Probably (like me) you weren't taught about money at school, and it wasn't really discussed openly at home, so don't expect yourself to be the expert. But here's the good news. You don't need to be an expert! Phew, I know, a palpable sigh of relief. All you need to do, is take a deep breath and start the conversation and that is exactly what this book is going to help you to do.

Money Confidence is a tool in your life confidence toolbox. It is no exaggeration that if you can successively navigate money, this will be one of the most important tools you have, to navigate life. Confidence and self-mastery, come as a result of many things and creating a confident relationship with money is one of the key elements. Money is never about just the numbers. It would be simple if that were the case. It's about beliefs, behaviours, emotions, identity and the action, we do or don't take as a result. It's the consequences of those actions and taking responsibility for them.

For our Teens, this time in their life, is a time when they are starting to define who they actually are. They are developing their own sense of identity, their own social circle, their own interests and even their values around what is important to them. And money plays a role in ALL of that.

Having the knowledge about how to make, manage and grow your money isn't just a skill, it's a superpower, have no doubt about that. It can mean the difference between living from payday to payday, having 'too much month left at the end of their money' and having the freedom to choose the kind of life they really want to be living. And the sooner your Teen can start to develop and nurture this mindset, the better. Where Mindset goes Money Grows®

What you'll learn in this book. This book is your guide to talking to your Teen about money. It will support you to have the conversations that matter and to work together to understand money in a way that's simple, practical and relatable. Yes, this book will cover the basics, like budgeting, saving and investing, but it will also cover what drives the behaviours and emotions around how we 'do' money. We will look at the 'why' behind the stories we tell ourselves when it comes to money, particularly around the actions that we take.

Together we will go on a journey, one where we explore the importance of saving, the impact of spending money on things we don't really need and how you can work together with your Teen to help them start thinking about money as a tool for their Future Self and not just something in the here and now.

This book is full of real-life examples, exercises to practice together and prompts to open the conversations between you and your Teen.

How to use this book. For parents, this book will give you the confidence to face the conversations you want and need to have with your Teen head on, in a way that feels open, natural and not awkward. You'll find practical advice on how to introduce certain topics, encourage discussions and here is a big bonus… you will find yourself learning alongside your Teen, if you are unfamiliar with certain areas of money management and the psychology around money.

There will be exercises and prompts throughout the book designed for both parents and teens. I suggest you pause and take the time to complete each one, as this is all about building the momentum in your money conversations. This will also help to create a habit, that you feel supports you to move forward on a regular basis. It is this that will not only increase your knowledge but skyrocket your confidence too.

There are no tests to complete, there is no right or wrong, this is a journey of exploration for you and your Teen, and I want you both to feel excited about what is to come.

The conversation starts now. Money talks, whether you like it or not. The earlier as parents we accept that and start to tune in and take control of the conversation, the better we and our Teens will be prepared for whatever life throws at them and you. So, whether you're a parent who's ready to give your child a financial head-start, or a Teen who wants to know more about money, this book is here to provide guidance for those conversations that count.

Are you ready? Of course you are!

CHAPTER 1
STARTING THE MONEY CONVERSATION

Let me start by asking you a question. 'Why did you buy this book?' I suspect it is because you want to be having conversations with your Teen about money. But because no one had those conversations with you when you were younger, you are at a loss as to where to start.

You are possibly blaming yourself for not encouraging these conversations about money more openly with your Teen. Perhaps you feel shame around not knowing more about money yourself. And as a parent, you feel responsible and worried about how your child can nurture a successful relationship with money, if you are their role model.

Stop.

Stop right now. Stop being so hard on yourself because you have done your best, with the limited information you were given about money, when you were a teen. Let's break this down further.

I would hazard a guess that like me, you were not taught about money at school. There was little if any discussion during lessons about budgeting, saving and investing and even less said about credit, debt and how to manage your money effectively.

I would also hazard a guess, that conversations around money did not happen at home either. Your parents may have said it was rude to talk about money, that you shouldn't even question anyone about money and that money should never been discussed openly and publicly, because it was not polite.

So, given all this, why would you expect to be able to confidently, comfortably and openly talk to your children about something, when you have never had those conversations yourself?

I want you to start celebrating you. Celebrate that you have now created the awareness about the need to have these conversations about money with your Teen.

Celebrate that you want them to have the knowledge and the know-how, that you didn't and that you went ahead and bought this book!
This book is going to change things up radically for you AND for your Teen. And that is all down to you. So, acknowledge and celebrate that today is day one of a new relationship with money for you, your Teen and the ripple effect that will happen as a result.

I want to dig deeper into your relationship with money - your 'money story' - as it is important to understand what is going on for you when it comes to money. This will allow you to help your Teen to understand their current relationship with money also. This is a pivotal piece, in order to create the kind of relationship with money, that really works, for both of you.

The purpose of this book, is not just so you can talk to your Teen about money. , It has a much bigger mission than that! I want you to radically transform your relationship with money too, because in doing so, you will be creating the evidence of what is possible for you while demonstrating this to your Teen too. Your Teen needs to be shown that change is possible, to encourage and motivate them to go on this journey with you.

Our relationship with money - our money mindset is formed by the age of seven. Yes seven. This shocks many people when I tell them this. I have lost count of how many times I have been asked, "But how can my money mindset be formed by the age of seven, when I don't remember having much awareness about money at that age?"

Of course, these comments are correct, none of us probably remember very much about money at such a young age, other than perhaps the money we were gifted by relatives for our birthday and at Christmas, etc. However, it's important to know that your money mindset, your very relationship with money, the thoughts and feelings you have about it, have nothing to do with your experiences of money, when you were younger, but everything to do with your parents and main caregivers and how they interacted and 'did' money.

I am going to get a little geeky for a moment. Up until the age of seven, children's brains spend a significant amount of time in the theta state. Theta waves are a type of brainwave that occur when we are in a deeply relaxed, meditative or drowsy state, which is often associated with creativity, intuition and our subconscious. This state occurs most prominently in early childhood, specifically from birth to age seven, which is a crucial time for forming core beliefs and our mental programming.

During our early years, we spend a significant amount of time in the theta state and like sponges we are absorbing information about our environment and those living in that environment with us. This is the reason why children are highly impressionable during this phase, taking onboard not just what is taught directly to them, but also what they observe in terms of emotions, attitudes and behaviour and here's the kicker……especially about money. The theta state makes us, as children, particularly vulnerable to forming deep-seated beliefs about money, success, self-worth and self-confidence, which we absorb from our parents, grandparents and key caregivers, as well as cultural surroundings.

The theta state is linked to our subconscious and plays a vital role in how our early experiences shape the core of our money mindset. For example, if a child repeatedly hears phrases like 'we can't afford that' or 'money is the root of all evil,' witnesses financial stress at home, or experiences a change in lifestyle due to shifting financial circumstances, these factors can embed in their subconscious and influence their future relationship with money.

Even though the theta wave dominance decreases as we grow older, the beliefs and patterns that are formed during our early formative years, continue to influence how we think about ourselves in terms of our self-worth, the internal conversations we have with ourselves with regards to our value, which in turn impact our financial decisions and behaviours, unless we actively work to change them.

This is why it is key to understand your money story, because in doing so you can start to identify your own limiting beliefs around money… which is key, because as parents, we are the authors of our children's money story. And as you now know your Teen's money mindset, was formed by the time they were seven, as a result of your relationship with money.

But if you are now panicking, please don't. Our money mindset is not fixed, it can be changed and transformed, once we understand what we are working with, and this is what you are going to do now.

I invite you to reflect right now on your own money story. What are your first memories about money? Let me help you do this, by asking some key questions. You can either write these down in the space provided or use a journal to capture your answers.

1.   What did I learn about money growing up?
Reflect on the messages you received about money as a child. Were these messages empowering or limiting? Did your parents or main caregivers talk openly about money? What emotions, attitudes and behaviours can you remember observing? This is a first step in you identifying what your early programming was.

2.   How do I feel when I think about money?

When answering this question, pay close attention to the emotions that come up when you think about money. Don't avoid the emotion, actively lean into it, as this will reveal so much to you. Do you feel anxious, excited, inspired, motivated, guilty or scared? This will allow you to uncover any underlying emotional triggers you hold around money.

3.   What are my earliest memories of money?

Think back to your very first memory about money. This might be receiving pocket money, buying something for the first time, a relative giving you money and telling you to keep quiet about it, or hearing your parents arguing about money. Our early experiences often inform the basis of our money beliefs.

4. What are my beliefs about money?

This might feel tricky or confronting initially but can help uncover something deep-rooted that has impacted how you think and feel about money and yourself. Do you believe that money is abundant or scarce? Do you think wanting more money makes you greedy? Do you believe that you will never have more money than your parents did? Understanding these beliefs can help you to highlight limiting thoughts, which can influence your behaviours and habits.

5. How do I behave when I have additional money?

If you come into extra money, through a bonus, or unexpected windfall for example, think about how you act. Do you spend it without thought, save it, or feel uncomfortable having it and want to get rid of it? This can reveal your spending and saving habits, which can in turn lead to you making different, more empowering decisions.

6. How do you behave when you don't have enough money?

Think about how you react to financial stress. Do you bury your head in the sand and avoid thinking about it, panic and become like a headless chicken, or do you become solution-focused, take control and come up with a plan? How you react in times of financial difficulty can reveal how resilient you are in your relationship with money, or how anxious you are.

7. What is my biggest financial fear?

Some people can tend to catastrophise and worry about things that never happen. Did you know that 97% of what we worry about never actually happens. Identifying your biggest fear around money, such as losing it all, never having enough, your family going without, can reveal deep-seated fears and beliefs, which could be paralysing you, or holding you in constant fear, which affect your ability to make good financial decisions.

8. Do I deserve to be wealthy?

This is such a powerful question to ask yourself, to really understand if you truly believe you are deserving of financial success. Having feelings of not being worthy of success when it comes to money, can actually block you from achieving your financial goals.

9. How does money currently impact my feelings of self-worth?

Reflect on how you feel about yourself and if your own self-esteem is interlinked with how much money you have? Do you feel more valuable when you have more money or ashamed when you don't? Do you compare yourself unfavourably to others who appear to have more money than you? Understanding this will help you to start uncoupling the link between your self-worth and money.

10.   What is my biggest financial regret?

Experience is how we learn, however holding onto regret can prevent us from moving forward through fear of it happening again. Think about your past financial mistakes or opportunities you have missed, as this can help you to understand how and why. You might be holding onto guilt or fear, which may be impacting current money decisions.

These are the key questions I want you to answer right now. But if you are keen to delve deeper, there are a further ten questions at the end of the book in the 'Additional Resources' section.

It's important you are really honest with yourself when answering all the questions posed in this book, as this will help create the awareness of why you may not have been talking to your Teen about money so far and inform how your Teen could be thinking about money right now.

It is this awareness that will start to connect the two of you when you start the money conversation, because you will understand why they have developed the beliefs they have. If these are limiting beliefs, then this is the perfect opportunity to work together to transform both your and their beliefs.

A reminder: as parents, we are the authors of our children's money story. In the next chapter we will start to explore how you can help to rewrite that money story into one that works for both of you.

Reflection Question:

What are the specific money lessons you wish you had been taught as a Teen?

Discuss these with your Teen.

Write your thoughts here:

CHAPTER 2
THE IMPORTANCE OF MONEY CONVERSATIONS

I know I am fortunate to have grown up in a very positive home environment, where my two siblings and I were always encouraged to do and be our best. My mother would not allow me to ever lower my expectations for myself. I would say things like, "I'm going to do two A Levels", but my mother would always respond matter of factly, "No you are not, you are doing three." Another example, when I said I was going to college, my mum's reply was, "No you are going to university," at a time when none of the women in my family had gone to university.

Both my parents had the expectation that we should

work hard at school, go to university, get a job and climb the career ladder. I duly did as was expected of me, but I don't remember very many, if any real conversations about money.

I do remember my dad religiously checking his bank statements against his cheque book stubs on a monthly basis and paying off his credit card bill every month, but I don't remember any conversations about budgeting, saving, investing (other than the need to pay into a pension plan) or credit and debt.

As soon as I was old enough, I did get a part time job in Boots and Tesco (I was a hard worker even back then) and loved earning my own money. I did save and I remember being proud of the fact that I was able to buy myself everything I needed to go to university out of my own funds. However, my approach to saving was short term and not particularly goal focused, more 'I want it, how can I ensure I can have it?'

This lack of real knowledge about money and the power

it can have over you, when you don't a) understand money practically and b) don't understand your own relationship with money, became very apparent during my 2nd year at university, when the credit card applications started to come through the post. I can remember opening up the envelopes and seeing how much money (debt!) I was being offered, for what appeared to be a very small amount of money I had to pay back each month. I didn't think to read the small print, where details of the Annual Percentage Rate (APR) were, because I simply did not know or understand about these things. All I saw was, 'easy money' being offered to me on a plate.

So, what did I do? Yes, you guessed it, I applied and due to the two part time jobs I had at university, I was accepted for a credit card, no issues at all. Happy days, or so I thought at the time.

Back then I had a very extravagant relationship with money, it was there to fund my wants and not my needs. I was fortunate my needs were met via the money I received from my parents and the two part time jobs I had, but I wanted more... the more being a trip to Marks & Spencer's on a Friday evening, to splash out on food and drinks I did not need, but absolutely wanted. Was it a status thing? Yes, sadly I think so. All funded by 'Mr. Credit Card'.

I saw absolutely no harm in it at all. I stayed within my credit limit (although was adding to my balance on a regular basis) and paid the required monthly amount on time. But it was the minimum monthly amount... because I had no clue that whilst this meant what I was paying back was small in the grand scheme of things, it meant interest (at pretty high rates) was being added, without me really being consciously aware. I was the credit card company's dream customer because I used the card, I kept to the agreement, but in a way that meant I was adding more and more interest to what I owed them. Why? Because I had absolutely no knowledge of how credit cards worked, because it had never been explained to me.

I was unconsciously incompetent but happy in my bubble of visiting Marks & Spencer's whenever I needed a dopamine hit, provided in the food aisles...

Fortunately, there is no sad ending to this story, other than the money wasted when I eventually woke up and realised how stupid my spending habits were and how much those unnecessary trips to said upmarket shop were costing me. But this was after I graduated, so goodness knows how much I had paid in interest over this time. When I realised, I actually cut up the card, started to overpay each month and eventually cleared the balance down to zero.

I can't exactly remember when the penny dropped (but it was well after I finished university), that the balance I had owed on my credit card, was actually debt. I had never made that connection, partly because credit card companies and indeed society as a whole, had educated me to think that paying for things in this way was OK. It was acceptable and even to be encouraged, because it allowed us to have things we wanted and not just what we needed.

I was lucky. The penny did eventually drop and my graduate salary allowed me to pay back every penny I owed quite quickly. However, I was a student in a very different time, before mobile phones, before social media, before consumer culture was really a 'thing'. Today is very different and there are so many more ways now that our Teens are being influenced; comparing what they have to what others have (supposedly). If we do not educate them on the downside of money, credit and debt, then the end to their story could be very different and this is why, as parents, it is our job to talk to our Teens about money.

We cannot expect others to do this on our behalf, because schools just don't have the time or resources to do so. One hour, once a year, is just not going to cut it. It is down to us to have these conversations and to have these conversations now.

Let me break this down even further, by having money conversations with your Teen, you will be:

Breaking the silence

Yes, we know that money is still often seen as a taboo subject in many families. However, something is only taboo if you accept that this is the case.

Avoiding money conversations leads to financial ignorance, which simply continues a lack of understanding from generation to generation. You are choosing to break this cycle; to remove the fear of judgement or worry that you don't have the right knowledge. You are choosing to break the silence that has existed for far too long. I want you to acknowledge this and to celebrate what you are doing, for yourself, for your family and for generations to come.

You will be supporting your Teen to avoid financial struggles in their future and equipping them with essential skills they will continue to use for the rest of their lives.

Normalising money talk at home

Starting these conversations around money now and

continuing to do so regularly, will lead to them becoming a natural part of family life. Encouraging questions and curiosity in our children should be welcomed, as this is how they learn, and creating an environment where they feel comfortable to ask questions about money will serve them well in all areas of their lives.

This creates self-confidence, which leads to Money Confidence, which leads to confidence in all aspects of your Teen's life. When money is no longer treated as a forbidden or off-limits topic, we are encouraging our Teens to feel comfortable asking questions and making informed decisions. Having money conversations openly will lead to the creation of a safe, judgement free environment, which will lead to more open and honest conversations.

It does not have to be difficult to start these conversations. You can normalise them by discussing the household budget together, explaining the different bills that need to be paid, explain how bills are paid, or even talking about the different decisions that can be made whilst doing the weekly shop.

Ask your Teen what they want to know about money

Starting the conversation can be as easy as asking your Teen what they want to know. They will have a number of questions they are keen to talk through with you, but please don't feel you need to have all the answers; you don't.

Some of your Teen's questions may be very practical, such as what a mortgage is, or when can they open a bank account of their own. You will have your own experience here and be able to answer these questions easily. However, there may be questions such as 'What exactly is an ISA?', or 'What is the best savings account?' that you might not feel so comfortable or confident answering, so simply tell your Teen you are not certain of the answer, but that you will either ask a trusted advisor, or do the research together to find the answer.

You really don't have to feel responsible for knowing it all. For example, if your Teen came to you and asked you to recite the whole of the periodic table, I am sure you would not feel shame or embarrassment about not being able to do so. Therefore why should you feel differently about not having all the answers to questions about money?

In being honest with your Teen and admitting you don't know the answer, this demonstrates that as adults we don't know everything and that it's OK to ask for help or how to find the answer for yourself. This again creates confidence helping them to feel comfortable enough to ask questions in the first place. Which in itself is a life skill.

Very often as adults, because we weren't encouraged to ask questions as children, or we felt embarrassed that we didn't understand something when our peers did, we have gone through life finding certain things hard. We may now feel too ashamed to address that lack of knowledge, because by this stage we feel we should already know it and now it's too late to ask (it's not too late, by the way!). We can ensure our Teens never feel like this, by encouraging them to ask questions, not feel shame at not having all the answers.

Financial knowledge is a journey, not a destination

How much have financial transactions changed since we were our children's age? Cheque books are a thing of the past, mobile phones and contactless payments are the method of choice and cash being given as a gift, is becoming more and more rare. We have all forms of digital currencies, many transactions happening online and not in person. This shift to a more digital and cashless society means that the financial landscape is continuously evolving and with it, so must our knowledge.

Our children are growing up in a world where mobile phone apps can manage their savings, investments can be made at the tap of a screen, and cryptocurrencies are part of everyday conversations. Yet, this convenience brings new challenges, like understanding digital security, managing online spending and navigating the complexities of virtual currencies. As parents, we need to stay informed, not just to keep up with these changes for ourselves, but to help our children develop the financial literacy and critical thinking skills necessary to thrive in this ever-changing world.

This journey of learning is ongoing and by embracing it together, we can ensure our children have the tools they need to make informed financial decisions throughout their lives. But we must also ensure our children understand this is a continuing process, the evolution of money will continue and it is OK to keep learning. Learning is to be actively encouraged along with the confidence to ask questions, so they continue to be correctly informed.

This is a gift to give to our children and we should embrace it, as much for ourselves as we do for them.

Money is a tool, much like a Swiss Army Knife

It's important our children realise money is so much more than just paying bills. Much like a Swiss Army Knife, which has many tools attached to it and no singular purpose, money helps create independence, supports decision-making and enhances critical thinking. Having open conversations about money can help Teens see money as part of their armoury of tools, to help them to achieve their goals and ambitions and is not something to be afraid of or stressed about.

As with anything, the more information we have, the more assured we feel and the more solution-focused we become, and this absolutely applies to money. It is not about being overly positive, or present a false reality, it is about being armed with the facts and knowing what to do with them.

Very often in times of greatest stress it is our lack of understanding about a situation that causes us to feel overwhelmed. Imagine being very familiar with the workings of a car and you suddenly hear a noise and feel the power reducing, you pull over and because you have an idea of what is happening - you go into solution solving mode, as opposed to the panic you might feel if you knew nothing about the workings of your car and therefore stumped as to what the problem might be.

Not everyone needs to be a car mechanic, but everyone should understand the basics of how to manage their money and where to go to further enhance their knowledge and make their money work for them. For our Teens, this education starts with us, their parents, but we do not need to be money experts ourselves to support them. As parents, being open to the conversations, honest about where the gaps are in your knowledge, and being prepared to learn alongside your Teen, is more important than having all the answers.

Money conversations create trust

When you start to have conversations about money with your Teen, you are setting the example that it's absolutely OK to talk about this stuff.

You are demonstrating that, while some conversations can be uncomfortable to begin with, taking the first step to start them, showing vulnerability and modelling the right behaviour can positively influence your Teen. This, in turn, will encourage them not only to engage in uncomfortable conversations but also to develop a healthier and more confident attitude towards money. If you are a parent who is old enough to remember the characters 'Kevin and Perry' (if you don't remember them then I'd highly recommend you head to YouTube), Kevin was your archetypal Teen: sulky, moody and completely at odds with his parents. It's likely you will recognise these same teenage traits in your own Teen. However, it is important to persevere, to encourage your Teen to open up and talk to you about money, because deep down, they really want to know. They will have questions and very likely they will already believe certain things that are simply not true and now is your opportunity to fact check with them. There are many benefits to talking to your Teen about money, but at this stage in their lives, one of the biggest benefits is that it will build trust between the two of you. These conversations provide the best opportunity to really talk to each other, about goals, aspirations, worries, limiting beliefs and so much more. Don't be surprised if you are provided with an insight into a side of your child you just were not aware of, as very often it is their deepest desires, that our children choose not to reveal to us, out of their fear about how we might react. Now is the time to fully step up as parents and show our children we can support their wildest dreams.

What is the cost of not having the money conversation?

If I was given a pound every time someone said to me, "My parents didn't talk to me about money when I was growing up," I would be a very rich woman! What has the impact of not talking to children about money had on our society?

The answer to this question could warrant a complete chapter of its own, but you are already here because you want to talk to your Teen about money, so I am not going to preach to the converted. I am here to celebrate that decision. However, just in case you have any lingering doubts, let me give a quick snapshot of what not talking to children about money has done….

- It has created poor financial habits - 11.5 million people in the UK have less than £100 in savings, one in three have no savings at all and only 25% have savings that would cover three months' worth of essential outgoings, which is the minimum recommended amount (Yorkshire Building Society 2023).

- Personal debt is on the increase – as of 2023, UK Adults held £207.1 billion in consumer credit debt, including credit cards, overdrafts and person loans.
- Lack of pension provision - whilst the introduction of auto-enrolment has improved the number of people paying into a workplace pension, research has shown around one in three UK adults are at risk of not having enough saved for retirement.
- Financial insecurity - research by the Joseph Rowntree Foundation found that around 19% of UK workers live in households classified as 'in-work' poverty, with their wages unable to cover essential living costs. Many families have little to no financial buffer.
- Planning for the future - a report by HSBC found that 37% of UK adults have no long-term financial plans and only half have made any plans for retirement. This lack of planning contributes to financial instability (and stress) later in life.

While parents not talking to their children about money cannot be solely blamed for the country's current financial issues, it is undoubtedly a contributing factor. Many adults have been ill-served by both the absence of money conversations at home and the lack of financial education in schools.

Research by Go Henry in 2023 stated that if all children were taught financial literacy from a young age, by 2050 this would add a further £200 billion to the UK economy… I can't think of a better reason to have the conversation with your Teens now, so they can benefit from this financial uplift as they go through their lives.

Reflection Question

Reflect on a money conversation you haven't had with your Teen and commit to starting that conversation this week. Make this a solid commitment by putting it in your calendar, as this increases accountability.

Note down potential questions you would like to ask and think about how to start the conversation in a way that opens the door for further conversations in the future. You've got this!

_____
_____
_____
_____
_____
_____
_____
_____
_____
_____

CHAPTER 3
BUILDING MONEY CONFIDENCE – FOR YOU AND YOUR TEEN.

Let me start by giving a definition for what Money Confidence actually is. It is the ability to make informed, empowered financial decisions with clarity and self-assurance. It involves having a positive mindset about money, understanding key financial concepts and trusting your capacity to manage, save and invest effectively, even when faced with financial challenges. It is not about knowing EVERYTHING there is to know about money - there are plenty of experts out there - but it is about knowing what you need to know to make the right decisions for you about money. This is something everyone should want for themselves and for their families and I can assure you, it is absolutely possibly for you and your children to create real and lasting Money Confidence.

What many people fail to understand, is how interlinked money and decision-making are with self-worth.

Self-worth is at the heart of a confident relationship with money; and what is at the heart of creating self-worth? Confidence in yourself.

Money Confidence comes as a result of self-confidence and not the other way around. If you do not have a confident relationship with yourself, you are not going to be able to have a confident relationship with money. Self-confidence is the key to Money Confidence.

So how do you create self-confidence? Creating self-confidence is not an overnight thing, it is a gradual process that involves building up trust in your own abilities and capabilities. It involves developing and maintaining a positive mindset, being open to creating change and taking action to strengthen your sense of self-worth.

So, what steps can you take to achieve this?

- Start by acknowledging your strengths and achievements. It is important to regularly reflect on what you're good at and celebrate all your successes, both big and small. By recognising your achievements this lays the foundation for self-competence and self-belief and seeing all the evidence that you have and are creating, to reinforce this.

- Set yourself small but achievable goals and if there are any big tasks, break these down into manageable steps, which avoids overwhelm, as you move towards them. Doing this will boost your confidence and create further self-evidence that you are capable of handling challenges and coming through them successfully.
- Develop a positive mindset. Our sub-conscious can be responsible for that inner self talk which holds us back. It is vital to retrain those thoughts into positive ones that support what you want to achieve and the actions you need to take as a result. Focus on what you can do, rather than what you can't and be kind to yourself in those moments of doubt. Doubt is normal, we all have it. It's how we deal with it, that counts.
- See mistakes as opportunities to learn and grow, this step is key not just for us as adults and

parents, but to instil in our children also. Failure is part of growth, we tend to learn from what we get wrong, not what we get right. Accepting mistakes and setbacks and viewing them as opportunities to learn and improve, are the real keys to progress.

- Growth happens outside your comfort zone, so gradually take on challenges that stretch you beyond your comfort zone. As you do the things that make you feel uncomfortable and start to see the results, this will educate your sub-conscious that you know what you are doing and this in turn will help to increase your confidence.

- Take good care of you, both inside and out. By taking care of your wellbeing, which includes both your physical and mental well-being, by paying attention to exercise, eating well, sleep, managing stress, (a dual healthy mind/healthy body approach), you contribute to a positive self-image.

- Surround yourself with cheerleaders. It is said we are the sum of the five people we spend most of our time with, therefore it is important these people support and encourage us. Surround yourself with supportive, positive people who believe in you and encourage your Teen to do the same.

I recommend focusing on these steps each and every day and taking note as your confidence becomes stronger and maintained for longer.

We have looked at how to grow your confidence and how developing a positive mindset is key, but I want to take this a step further and explore the importance of developing the right money mindset, specifically.

What is the role of mindset in developing Money Confidence

Beliefs about money can deeply impact what we believe is possible for us and in turn, the financial choices we make. Therefore, our beliefs can either be empowering or limiting, depending on whether or not those beliefs are positive or negative.

If you have empowering beliefs about money, you believe:

- There is always enough money, and you have the ability to ensure you will always have enough. This is an abundance mindset, which allows you to go for opportunities, invest in yourself and take calculated risks; having the confidence in yourself to make the right decisions. As a result, you are more likely to budget well, invest in your future and take a long-term view when it comes to decisions.
- Money is a tool, which enables you to achieve your goals and will support you in achieving the kind of life you want for yourself. You are not obsessed with money nor solely focused on it, you view it as something that can support you, provide security and help you to achieve independence. As a result, you are likely to focus on how money can support you to live your life in the way you choose and brings you joy.
- You are worthy of achieving financial success. This can lead to behaviour that encourages you to look for better opportunities, be confident in asking for pay rises or seek ways to grow your business. You are likely to get back up after a set

back and regard it as a lesson, rather than throw you permanently off course.

However, so many more people have limiting beliefs around money, which show up in the following ways:

- A belief that money is limited or scarce, which can lead to decisions that come from a place of fear, such as hoarding money, feeling uncomfortable spending money or totally avoiding risks. If you have a scarcity mindset you might avoid investment opportunities or remain in a job where you are undervalued. This can lead to being unable to create enough money to feel comfortable and confident about your ability to make the right decision.
- You may subconsciously sabotage your own financial success because you believe that money causes problems or is the 'root of all evil' and therefore avoid doing the things that could actually create financial stability. It is likely you avoid taking risks or become overly conservative

with money which also impacts the ability to create wealth.
- You may hold the belief that you can never make more than a certain amount of money or that you are not capable of managing big sums of money. This belief limits not only your ambition for yourself but also your willingness to look for new opportunities. This belief can cap income potential and therefore limit your ability to create financial independence.

Beliefs about money are usually deeply rooted in our childhood experiences, which is why it is so important to reframe negative beliefs. Empowering beliefs create internal confidence and motivation to make sound financial decisions based on evidence while limiting beliefs are just that; limiting. They hold us back from realising our full financial potential.

As parents, it is vital that we support our Teens to build their confidence, rather than focusing on what they don't know yet.

The teenage years are not easy. It is a time when hormones are all over the place, insecurities about how we look can be at an all-time high, we start to become more aware of our environment and more aware of what we don't know, rather than focusing on what we do.

This is why we need to be talking to our Teens about money because they will be starting to think about money in a more meaningful way than at any other time in their lives so far. As parents we want to ensure our Teens feel able to ask the questions they need to ask, to gain the knowledge that is going to help create their own confidence in terms of their relationship with money.

As part of the conversation, we need to reassure our Teens that financial mistakes are part of the learning process, however it is possible to mitigate many of these mistakes by opening up the communication channels between you and your child. You want them to feel coming to you is a safe and judgement free way for them to ask questions and to test their knowledge in a way that makes them feel valued and supported.

This may be the ideal time for you to share any mistakes you made with money when you were younger. This is to provide your Teen with the context that mistakes are normal and to ask for the right support when required. Depending on the age of your Teen, you could even take this as an opportunity to ask them what they would do differently had they been in your position. This allows the two of you to become solution-focused and to discuss the outcomes of different scenarios, providing your Teen with a real-life case study from which they can learn. Taking this opportunity for your Teen to learn from your past mistakes allows them to practise financial decision making in a safe but informed way. This will start to increase their own sense of self-confidence and increase their sense of trust in you, in helping them to learn from past mistakes.

The ideal way to support your Teen to build their confidence with money is by gradually introducing them to financial responsibilities as they grow. You can have a discussion for example, around giving them control over a portion of their finances e.g., a clothing allowance or managing their own savings account, to help them build independence. It is important to highlight to your Teen how you trust them to manage their money effectively but also reassure them that you are here should they need you.

"Let's Talk!"

Reflection Exercise

Money Confidence Journal

As a parent, you want to open up a permanent channel of communication between you and your Teen and this next exercise will provide the opportunity for your Teen to practise their money skills and at the same time share what they are learning with you.

Step 1.

Encourage your Teen to start tracking their financial choices in a notebook or journal. Just what they are spending their money on at this stage.

Step 2.

Together with your Teen create one short-term financial goal, for example to save £20 for a new Xbox game and one long-term goal, for example save £100 for a new pair of trainers.

Encourage them to think about why they have chosen

these goals and how they plan to achieve them.

Step 3.

Now ask your Teen to keep a record of the spending, earning and saving decisions in their notebook or journal. Depending on the time scales you both agree on, each day or week, your Teen should write down:

1. What money they spent and why they chose to spend it in that way; reflecting on whether it was 'a want' or 'a need'. For example buying a new 'skin' for their PC game; did they need to have it or was it purely something they wanted to have?

2. Did that decision positively or negatively impact the two goals they agreed with you?

3. How did the decision make them feel? Did it support them in achieving their goals or hinder?

4. What will they do next time e.g., next time, I'll plan before I spend.

Step 4.

Track progress over time. After several entries in their journal, ask your Teen to look back and reflect on:

- What patterns they notice e.g., I make better decisions when I wait and think about the purchase, rather than rushing in.
- How has their confidence grown? E.g., I feel more in control and responsible for my decisions when I budget for the things I really want.

Step 5.

- Do the same exercise yourself and share some of the journal entries with your Teen. As a parent you can model your own reflections and help your Teen to identify their progress.
- It is important that you as a parent demonstrate to your Teen this is a judgement free zone and an opportunity to ask questions and to learn. It is really important to encourage open discussion about what both you and your Teen are learning through this process.

This exercise is the ideal opportunity to help your Teen build their money confidence by allowing them to see their progress and not feel judged learning from their and your experiences, as well as being able to see they're growing their financial skills. It also encourages a healthy conversation between parents and teens about money choices and in doing so reinforces the idea that building Money Confidence is always an ongoing journey.

CHAPTER 4

UNDERSTANDING BASIC MONEY CONCEPTS TOGETHER

My whole premise for writing this book is to overcome the belief held by many parents that talking to their Teen about money is difficult. One of the biggest misconceptions parents have is that in order to talk about money they need to have all the answers or be some kind of financial expert. Nothing could be further from the truth.

Let me reassure you; you don't need to be a world-class economist or understand every detail about shares, property or cryptocurrency, to have meaningful conversations about money with your Teen. In fact, these things aren't even the most important part of financial literacy at this stage in their lives.

What really matters is the mindset you help your Teen develop when it comes to money. The ability to be curious, open, and willing to ask questions is far more important than knowing all the technical details. Why? Because financial knowledge changes all the time. New tools, trends and opportunities emerge constantly, but the ability to learn, ask questions and seek answers is timeless.

As a parent, it is your job to encourage curiosity over perfection. What if instead of worrying about teaching your Teen all the right answers, you focused on helping them ask the right questions…

- Encourage them to question what they hear and see about money in their daily life, whether it's on social media, from friends or even at school or college.
- Encourage them to explore how money affects the world around them, such as understanding

why they get a certain amount of allowance or pocket money and how interest works on their savings account.

- Encourage your Teen to be open to learning together, make it clear that you don't have to know everything, instead say, "Let's work it out together." How empowering is that for both of you?

By modelling curiosity, you show your Teen that money isn't something to be frightened of or intimidated by, it's something to be explored, step by step.

I invite you to become comfortable with saying, "I don't know", when it comes to money. There is real value in being comfortable with saying that you don't know but you want to find out. This teaches your Teen a vital life skill; they don't need all of the answers at once, but they need the confidence to find out.

This also shifts the pressure off you as a parent. How good does that feel? Instead of feeling like you need to have all the money 'know how', you're simply positioning yourself as a guide, which is helping your Teen develop their own money story.

One of the most powerful things you can do as a parent is show your Teen that talking about money doesn't have to be formal or stressful. You don't need spreadsheets or detailed financial reports to start the conversation, it can be as simple as:

- Ask your Teen what they think about something they bought recently. Was it worth it? Why/why not?
- The 'art of the possible' is a really encouraging concept that supports your Teen to push the outer limits of what they think is currently possible for them and expands their horizon in terms of what they would like to achieve if everything were aligned for them.
- Encourage your Teen to think about their future goals and how money can support them in

achieving those goals. A simple question like, 'what would you like to save for?', can really open up a conversation about the 'art of possible' for your Teen and encourage them to reflect on what they want.

- This conversation will expose their own limiting beliefs right now and allow the two of you to position how your Teen can really push the boundaries of what they believe is possible for them.
- Work out a plan together on how to achieve it - and go for it. It is also your opportunity as a parent, to do the same for yourself.
- Start sharing an everyday money moment from your life such as, 'I've just paid the electricity bill, let's chat about what it covers', or, 'I have set up a direct debit for our council tax, let's have a chat about this payment.'

These small casual conversations around money build confidence and comfort for your Teen. They learn that it's OK to talk about money without feeling overwhelmed. They start to realise that money is just another part of everyday life, that they can start to understand with practice and ease.

There are just four topics your Teen needs to be aware of right now and these are budgeting, goal setting, saving and investing. Anything more complicated is unnecessary.

We will explore these four topics in more detail in the next few chapters, but right now you just need to be open about learning together.

It's important to communicate that you are both still learning, and that's absolutely fine! Money conversations should not be a one-way street where you're delivering lectures. Instead take the opportunity to explore new topics and trends together because, believe you me, new topics and new trends will keep on coming.

- If your Teen is curious about investing, you could read an article or watch a video on how the stock market works together. YouTube, TikTok and Instagram are full of them and you can both discuss your thoughts afterwards.

- If your Teen wants to discuss something they've heard about cryptocurrency or an online business, have that discussion. Neither of you have to be an expert to start critically thinking about how these things work. Talk, explore and learn together.

The key thing I want to stress is that money conversations don't need to be difficult, daunting or anything to be afraid of. The goal is simple: to encourage curiosity, openness, honesty and the ability to question and learn together. This is what will set your Teen up for a life of financial success.

Reflection Exercise

On the next page list three money-related topics that you and your Teen could explore together. How could this shared learning experience strengthen their confidence in asking questions and seeking answers?

CHAPTER 5
SETTING FINANCIAL GOALS

Goal setting is where teaching our children about money should ideally begin, because it gives them a clear sense of purpose and direction with their money.

When children understand how to set and achieve financial goals, they are learning that money is a tool to help them create the life they want. By starting with goal setting, we teach our children to think beyond immediate spending and encourage them to plan for the future, whether it's saving for something they want, building an emergency fund - or as I prefer to say, a soft landing fund - or starting to think about investing in their future.

This lays the foundation for discipline, patience and confidence in managing their money both in the short term and long term.

Financial goals give us all something to aim for, they give money a purpose, rather than simply being something we spend without a plan. They create motivation around the action we need to take and why, which in turn helps us to make good decisions or not.

By encouraging your Teen to set goals, you are empowering them to think about what they really want and plan how to make it happen. Setting goals will take them out of the here and now and transport them to a place they want to be.

It doesn't matter how small the goals are initially, the important thing is to set the goals, as that creates a whole new dynamic around the art of the possible. Yes, I make no apology for coming back to this theme again, because as parents, we really should be encouraging our children and in particular our Teens, to believe anything is possible for them.

See it, believe it, achieve it.

Encourage your Teen to set three types of goals: short-term, medium-term and long-term

Short-term goals – These are goals that your Teen can and wants to achieve in just a few weeks or months e.g., saving for concert tickets, new trainers or a new computer game.

Medium-term goals – Goals for the next one to five years e.g., saving for driving lessons, a new laptop or a first holiday with friends.

Long-term goals – Goals that take five or more years to achieve e.g., saving for a car, a deposit on a house, or even retirement (yes, it's never too early to plan ahead).

Exercise

Sit down with your Teen and ask them to identify one of each type of goal and discuss how they could go about planning for each one. Then you do the same.

Encourage your Teen to set SMART goals, not just arbitrarily plucking a goal out of the air.

SMART stands for:

Specific - A goal should be clear and detailed, outlining exactly what you want to achieve, like saving £100 for a new pair of trainers.
Measurable - A goal needs to be trackable so you can see progress, such as setting aside £10 each week until you reach your goal.
Achievable - The goal must be realistic and within your ability and control, like saving a manageable amount from your allowance or part-time job.
Relevant - The goal should align with your values and needs, ensuring it's something meaningful and important to you.
Time-bound - A goal needs a clear deadline, like reaching your savings target in three months, to stay focused and motivated.

So, the next step, once your Teen (and you - this is the perfect opportunity for you to be modelling the right behaviour for your Teen) has their short, medium and long-term goals, is to ensure they fit the SMART framework.

This adds specificity and accountability to the process and encourages responsibility. This further adds to the feeling of confidence that your Teen feels about taking control of their relationship with money and should also create a sense of excitement, as they start to commit to their Future Self.

What next?

Once the goals have been created, the next thing to do is to break those goals down into smaller actionable steps. This can stop the goal from feeling too big, or overwhelming. Feeling overwhelmed can lead to procrastination or avoiding doing the very thing that needs to be done to achieve the goal in the first place. Encourage your Teen to talk through with you, how they can create a clear plan and how creating smaller milestones will help them to maintain motivation.

Also encourage them to come up with ideas on how to achieve the required steps, as this not only promotes shared learning, but will allow your Teen to see that you are there to support and encourage them. This shared experience can be immensely rewarding and lead to more open conversations in other areas of your Teen's life also.

Let's look at an example. If the goal is to save £500 for their first holiday with friends and they have 10 months before the planned trip takes place. Break this down into £50 per month and then into £12.50 per week. £12.50 will feel far less daunting and achievable to your Teen than £50 and you can then also discuss ways of saving that money, which feels empowering and motivating too.

Do the same with each of their goals, or simply choose one to begin with, if more than one feels too much right now. Work through the process of breaking that goal down into smaller steps, creating a timeline for each step.

I would really encourage you to work together on a step-by-step savings or earning plan for one of your Teen's goals and discuss how they feel about this goal. Helping them to feel emotionally connected to their goal, is a helpful way to ensure they are committed to it. Also speaking to them about delayed gratification could be really helpful right now. Explaining how not buying something now, could ensure they are able to achieve their goal, in the timeline they set, or even achieve it more quickly.

Understanding the concept of delayed gratification also encourages responsible decision making in your Teen. They start to understand the impact of their spending. This allows them to make decisions based on how much they want to achieve their goal vs the impulse purchase they want right now. Allowing them the space to make that decision and understand the consequences, again promotes that all important confidence in their own decision making and their money confidence too.

The power of prioritising goals

Understanding the power of delayed gratification cannot be underestimated, as this really does provide teens with the knowledge and experience of what will happen, based on a decision they make. Not all goals can be achieved at once, so it is important to decide which goals are more important and in what order. This can be based on wants and needs and examining the motivation behind setting those goals in the first place. For example, if your Teen has a goal to save for a new phone and a trip with friends, have the discussion on how to prioritise savings for each. This not only encourages solution-focused thinking but also helps them to see money as a resource, which requires active management.

This is a great opportunity to discuss, as a family, which of your goals are the most important and what the priorities are over the next few months, or even longer. This open and shared conversation helps create a warm and encouraging atmosphere where teens feel empowered to approach discussions about money without fear or intimidation.

Tracking goals and staying accountable

Encourage your Teen to regularly track how they are doing against the goals they have set and help them stay accountable. They can do this in a variety of ways, such as a notebook or journal, an app or spreadsheet. It doesn't matter how they do it, but it's important they do it, as this will help to maintain motivation, allow for input and advice if needed and provide a real sense of accomplishment when the goal is achieved.

You could decide to track progress together or simply ask your Teen to give you a regular update. Remember to maintain a judgement-free zone should they go off track and support if required to get back on track.

You could agree to set up weekly or monthly 'money meet-ups', to review the goal against progress. Discuss what is working and what is not and how your Teen can stay on track.

If you are working towards your own SMART goals at the same time (and I certainly encourage this), then you could ask for ideas from your Teen at the same time, which will also feed into their sense of confidence too.

Let's Talk!

Reflection Exercise

Discuss with your Teen, how creating SMART goals for their money makes them feel and how they would like your support in achieving them.

Notes

CHAPTER 6
THE POWER OF BUDGETING (SOFT LANDING FUND)

Why budgeting is a superpower

Budgeting has the perception for many of being something that people with little money do but let me let you in on a not-so-secret secret… budgeting is a superpower. It's not just for those with little resources; it's the very tool that has allowed the most financially successful individuals to build and maintain their wealth.

Budgeting is often associated with restriction, something that limits our freedom to spend. In reality, and here is one of my favourites reframes, budgeting is what gives you freedom. It is the foundation upon which financial confidence is built. When you budget, you are not limiting yourself, you're empowering yourself. By knowing your numbers, you are taking control of where your money goes, rather than wondering where it has gone.

Wealthy people don't become and remain wealthy by accident. Behind every successful business owner, entrepreneur, investor or financially savvy person there is a very clear and intentional plan. They know exactly what is coming in and what's going out. More importantly, they allocate their resources in ways that creates future wealth and supports them to build their future intentionally, rather than sabotaging it. Budgeting is not about having less – it's doing more with what you have.

Budgeting is about knowing your numbers and understanding how to use them effectively. In his book, *The Big Leap*, Gay Hendricks highlights that 60% of big lottery winners end up either back where they started financially or worse off. One of the biggest reasons for this is their inability to budget and manage their money, often leading to overspending, overcommitting, and failing to plan for long-term financial security.

Fundamentally, they failed to understand how to budget, and it cost them a significant amount of money.

I want you to think of budgeting as the blueprint for you and your Teen to achieve your financial goals. It doesn't matter how much you or they are currently earning, the principle of budgeting remains the same. It is a clear plan for your money, enabling you both to achieve bigger things. The wealthy understand that money is a tool and budgeting is how they utilise that tool with real precision, not only to meet their needs today, but to secure opportunities for tomorrow.

When you think about budgeting in this way, doesn't it make it feel much more exciting and inviting? It's not about restriction at all, it's about creating a plan and being intentional with that plan.

The real secret is that budgeting is not a reflection of how much money you have right now, it's a reflection of how much control you have over your financial life. Supporting your Teen to start creating the habit of having a budget now, is empowering them to see this as a tool to aid their financial confidence and not to restrict them.

Now that you understand the power of budgeting, I want to break it down into three core components.

- Income
- Expenses
- Savings

These are your building blocks when it comes to creating a successful budget. When you learn how to manage these elements well, you are setting yourself and your family up for long-term financial success. How empowering does that feel!

Income – what money is coming in?

So, whether you are looking at your own budget (and modelling this for your Teen) or helping your Teen to understand theirs (or even doing it together!), income is the place to start with every budget. What money is coming in, either through a salary, wages, benefits, gifts or allowances? Identify it all, as the key is a get a clear picture on all sources of income that are coming in and **write them down**.

Now let me say something important here. For some people looking at their bank account and other sources of financial information can be hugely uncomfortable. So uncomfortable that they or even you, may avoid looking at these numbers at all. The numbers on your bank statement, credit card balance, or financial accounts are just that – numbers. They're not a reflection of your worth, intelligence, or potential. This is where many of us fall into a mental trap. We interpret these figures, as personal judgements, when in reality, they're neutral pieces of information and information upon which you can take action!

This discomfort often arises from the identity we attach to money. We might think, 'If I have less money, I have created a less successful life', or, 'If my savings aren't where they should be, I've failed' or, 'How can I expect to help my Teen develop a successful relationship with money, when I haven't managed that for myself.' But these are just stories we are telling ourselves, stories like these can stop us from taking control of our finances and stop us from helping those we really want to: our children and family.

A reminder: money is JUST a tool, and your current financial situation does not define you.

Our bank account is brilliant at leaving clues, we just have to be open to spotting and correctly interpreting what those clues mean and how we can use that information to our financial advantage.

We have to reprogramme what we think money is. Money is just a tool and neither you, nor your Teen's current financial situation are defined by it. It's simply a starting point and adopting budgeting as a behaviour, is the first step towards taking control, or regaining control. Irrespective of where you are right now.
If you are currently choosing to avoid looking at your finances, this will only serve to feed your anxiety. It is an endless vicious circle. The longer you avoid it, the scarier the idea of tackling and confronting your finances becomes. And I know you don't want this for

your Teen, do you?

Avoiding your bank account is like avoiding the weighing scales because you're afraid of the number you'll see. The number doesn't change just because you ignore it, but facing it is the first step toward taking ownership and creating a plan to make it one you feel confident about.

Whether you need to regularly get into the habit of reviewing your finances, or your weight, the process is very similar. Facing either of those numbers head on is the most empowering step you can take. By removing the emotional attachment to the number and seeing it for what it really is - information - you can begin to create a plan.

You will then be in a position to say… this is where I am. This is where I want to be. This is how I am going to get there.

You are taking back your power over those numbers, rather than letting them control you.

It may help you to ease into this process gently. And this is perfect. You don't have to do it all at once. Start small, make it simple, by looking at just one element of your finances to begin with. This could be your current account, or you may decide to track your spending for a week. This simple act of creating awareness and writing things down, will move you to a place of conscious decision making, which leads to further conscious decision making.

Gradually over time - but define that timeline if possible so you continue to see progress - you will build your confidence to assess the wider picture when it comes to your finances. If you do start to feel overwhelmed, involve a trusted friend or partner, a family member, or financial advisor, to support you. But whatever you do, don't stop. You have taken the biggest step; you have started, and you don't want to lose this momentum.

And when you feel comfortable and confident you have a plan you can stick to and will work for you, why not involve your Teen in this process too?

Depending on their age, they may already have

developed a real dislike for their own numbers and could be burying their head in the sand regarding the reality of their situation. This is the ideal opportunity for you to support them and speak to them about how to get comfortable with their 'information' and how to create a plan that works for them.

They are going to feel much more empowered and motivated to stick to a plan they can see will work for them, than to continue to do what they have been doing and avoid confronting the financial situation they may have found themselves in.

Remember, if up until now you have not been talking to your Teen about money, it is likely that no one has. So now is the opportunity for you both to learn together.

The first step, perhaps for both of you, is to understand what money is coming in and begin to really connect to your numbers. Then you can create a plan on how you will change those numbers to create the kind of life you want moving forward.

Income is the starting point for every budget. It's the

money that comes into the household. For parents, this includes salary or wages, whilst for teens it might be an allowance/pocket money, part-time job earnings, or initiatives like babysitting or cutting the grass for a neighbour. Start by writing down everything that is coming in and from where.

Encouraging your Teen to do this, helps them to understand that income is not endless and it needs to be managed wisely.

Expenses - what's going out?

Next in the process is to understand what commitments you have on a weekly or monthly basis. This of course will be very different for you as a parent, compared to your Teen.

For you they are likely to include mortgage or rent, utility bills, credit card/loan repayments, travel costs, shopping, clothes etc.

For your Teen, they may have no real expenses yet, or again age dependent, they may include things like mobile phone, socialising with friends, clothes, or even credit card repayments if they are over 18 (no judgement here, but at this age I hope not).

For budgeting to work, it's important to categorise all expenses into needs and wants.

- Needs are the essentials that you must provide for; housing, food, transport, utilities, debt repayment etc.
- Wants are the things you enjoy but are not essential to your survival, such as visits to Starbucks, new trainers, or the latest X box game.

Simply by creating these two categories, you can create a picture of what is important and what you really can do without. Not from the perspective of giving up something you enjoy, but from the perspective of being conscious about where your money goes and making a choice on how you decide to spend your money.

By encouraging your Teen to track their expenses, even

if limited right now, the sooner they will understand the difference between wants and needs and how to balance them, which in turn will lead to them becoming more financially responsible.

This can be a game-changer for both them and you, starting to approach money and how you spend it, from the perspective of choice and no longer feeling it has control over you.

However money never really had control over you. It was just your perspective.

Ask yourself the question – How do I feel knowing I have control over my money? And also, what changes for me, now I have control over my money?

These are great questions to also ask your Teen. Creating this level of awareness at their age, can really lead to a completely different journey for them, when it comes to their relationship with money.

It is not about restriction, although this may be necessary to achieve financial goals (more on this later).

It is about understanding you have choices and feeling empowered by those choices.

This creates a much healthier mindset in which to move forward. A mindset that puts you and your Teen in control of your financial future. And much more.

Savings – putting this first

So, this may surprise you... Do you know what one of the most important parts of a budget is? Ok, I may have given a teeny tiny clue in the title of this next section... savings!

This is game-changing in terms of helping you and your Teen to completely change how you approach your money and how conscious you are in terms of your behaviour with it. This means both you and your Teen, set aside an amount of your income for savings BEFORE you cover any of your other expenses.

Yes, you read that right. I am recommending that you set aside a certain amount of your money for savings, before any other money is deducted.

Savings can be used for short-term goals, such as building an emergency fund—or as I prefer to call it, a soft-landing fund - for unexpected expenses. This not only provides reassurance that you can cover unplanned costs without relying on debt but also helps develop a healthy habit of creating future savings for other financial goals.

Savings can also be used to achieve long-term goals like a holiday, driving lessons, a first car, higher education or even retirement. Even a small amount each month, can over time make a difference and it's really important to model this habit for your Teen.

Helping them to understand money isn't just about talking to them about money, it's also about modelling the right behaviour. Our children will often watch what we do and copy it, more than doing what we tell them…

It's vital to help them understand that saving isn't about deprivation, it's about making choices and creating financial security and freedom for the future.
As parents, we want to prepare our children for the real

world, particularly when it comes to managing money. In doing this, one of the most important things we can teach them about is delayed gratification. This is the ability to wait for something better, rather than giving into 'I want it now'. This is not always easy, especially when we live in a world of excessive consumerism and instant satisfaction, but understanding how to wait and more importantly, why to wait, can make a massive difference to their financial future.

What is delayed gratification?

Essentially, delayed gratification is making the conscious decision to wait for something bigger or more meaningful, instead of going for a quick win e.g., not purchasing a new pair of trousers, simply because they are on sale. Instead making the decision to save that money, because you want to have a weekend away with friends later in the year. Or deciding not to spend birthday money on a new video game, instead putting that money towards driving lessons or even saving for a car. It's about learning to become patient and to make decisions on behalf of your Future Self, rather than giving in to more immediate short-term desire.

As a parent, to be able to discuss this concept with your Teen is crucial, as it will help them understand the financial decisions they make today, can and will affect the opportunities they have in the future. The small purchases they consciously choose to not make now, rather than feel deprived, will lead to feeling empowered and making decisions that enable their future, rather than potentially limiting it.

Here are some reasons why I believe delayed gratification will help you have the conversation with your Teen:

- Helps save for bigger goals – when you practise delayed gratification, you're able to set money aside for bigger things that are really important to you. This may be a first car, college expenses, or even travelling. These are things that small impulse purchases don't offer and will mean more to your Teen, because they will have worked for them and waited. All this helps to create self-confidence and belief, which doesn't just impact their Future Self financially.

- Avoids debt – learning to wait can in turn prevent the need to turn to credit to fund your lifestyle at a later point in the future. Many people get into trouble because they want something immediately and use credit cards or loans to pay for it, then spend years paying it off. But, at what cost in terms of the interest? How much better could that money be spent on something meaningful, rather than servicing debt?
- Teaches self-control – life is full of decisions and many of them involve choosing between something that is fun and easy, or something that will lead to greater reward later. The second option isn't always fun, but it creates opportunities for increased fun at a later day. A good example of this is revising for exams. For most, it's not the most exciting way to spend time, but when you think about how you will feel on the day you get your results, the time invested in revising will be what leads to how you feel on the day about those results. So, learning to practise delayed gratification, doesn't

just benefit someone financially, but in many other ways too.
- Creates more freedom in the future - making smart decisions about money in the present, allows you to enjoy more freedom in the future. If you can save and wait for what you really want, quite simply you will have more options later. It doesn't matter if the goal is travelling, starting a business, or a plan to create peace of mind (and never underestimate how good this feels).

How can you model delayed gratification for your Teen?

I am sure you have heard of the saying, 'Do as I say and not as I do'? How often have you asked your child not to do something and they say, 'But I have seen you do it.' Our children model our behaviour, this is how they learn. Think back to when they were babies… they learnt to walk, because they watched you. They learnt how to eat, because they watched you. If you think back, there will be many examples of when your child has mimicked what you have already done, because quite simply, this is how they and we all learnt, from watching our role models… who are usually our parents when we are children.

Why should this be any different when it comes to learning about money? The truth is it is not any different at all.

If as parents, we want to teach our children about money and the importance of delayed gratification when it comes to achieving our financial goals, then we must model this behaviour for them.

Here are some practical suggestions on how you can model this behaviour and how you can work on this as a family:

- Set financial goals together – Over dinner, or another time when you are all together, talk about some of the things that you would like to achieve as a family. This may be saving for a holiday, a new kitchen, or whatever collectively you can feel invested in. By planning this together, in terms of how much it is going to cost, what you need to save, what choices you will need to make to achieve the goal, this will demonstrate how waiting for something bigger really does pay off.

- Use the 24-hour rule – Before buying something you want, particularly if it is not something you need, wait for 24 hours. Tell your Teen what you are doing and why and suggest they do the same the next time they go to make a purchase. Then ask them to share that experience with you.

- Choose experiences over things - Talk to your Teen about the cost of impulse purchases - like clothes never worn or trendy gadgets gathering dust - and compare what that money could have been spent on instead, such as a holiday or a memorable adventure.

- Talk about the financial trade-offs you have made - involve your Teen in the decisions you are making, in order to work towards a certain financial goal. For example, you may decide to not eat out for a month. Explain to your Teens how that money is going towards the goal you have agreed as a family and how this short-term decision, will allow you and the family to be looking forward to achieving the goal.

- Use a reward system – Delayed gratification does not mean missing out or that you can't celebrate milestones along the way. Agree together what those milestones will be and how you will reward yourself as a family when you achieve them. The rewards don't have to involve spending any money and could be as simple as a family film night, a family favourite meal, or something else that will keep you all motivated towards achieving your goal. This will demonstrate to your Teen that while waiting is important, it doesn't mean you can't enjoy yourself along the way.

How can you create a budget that works for your household

I hope I have demonstrated throughout this book so far, that creating a budget is not about being restrictive. It's about being intentional and conscious regarding decisions about your money, aligning your money with the goals you have for your life and encouraging your Teen to do the same thing. Not only through the conversations you are now having with them, but how you are modelling the right behaviour too.

So, let's set some clear priorities on how to set a budget that works for you as a family. Some of these I have covered already in this chapter, but below I have set it out in a framework I call 'Let's Create Smart Thinking Around Money'.

- **L**ist your income and expenses – Know your numbers now and decide on what you want them to look like in the future. Be honest and thorough, as sometimes the small expenses can quickly add up, but go unnoticed.
- **C**ategorise and prioritise – Break your expenses into two categories: needs or wants. Then ask yourself, which of these are non-negotiable and which ones can you proactively decide that you no longer need and can start putting towards your 'future number'. Make sure a portion of

your money is immediately saved every month, as a priority.

- **S**et clear goals – Ensure your budget aligns with your family's goals and that you are all clear on what those goals are, the cost of achieving them and the part each family member must play in achieving that goal. Remember the goals must be SMART (specific, measurable, realistic and time bound) and at the same time ensure your Teen is setting their own goals also.
- **T**rack and review – A budget is for life and not just a one-time goal, it should be a living document that evolves as your needs and circumstances change. Develop the habit of regularly reviewing your budget and involve your Teen (and other family members) in the process. Use this as the opportunity to discuss how things have gone in the month, what went well and what could be adjusted.
- **M**ake it a family commitment – There is no better way to talk to your Teen about money, than involving them in actual decision making around the budget process. It is not only the

ideal way to teach them about money, but it also adds a sense of responsibility. Take the opportunity to sit down together to review the family budget and let them see how you make decisions about spending, saving and prioritising. They may also come at it with a fresh perspective that you may not have already considered.

When teens see budgeting in action, they will realise that it's not about limitation but having control and freedom to achieve their financial goals. It's about the choices they make.

And as Benjamin Franklin said, 'Tell me and I forget, teach me and I may remember, involve me and I learn.'

"Let's Talk!"

Exercise - Budget check-in

Sit down with your Teen and review your budget together. Ask:

Are there any areas in the budget where we could spend less and save more for something important?

Question to Discuss with Your Teen-

How could sticking to a budget help us reach our bigger financial goals faster?

This encourages your Teen to think about the power of budgeting and how small adjustments can lead to long-term rewards.

Notes

CHAPTER 7

NAVIGATING DIGITAL MONEY AND ONLINE SPENDING

The rise of digital money has fundamentally changed the way we manage and spend our money. From mobile payments and contactless cards to online shopping and digital wallets, money is no longer something we physically see or handle. For teens growing up in the new digital area, the convenience and speed of digital transactions can make it easy to spend money, without fully realising the impact.

As I previously mentioned, I can remember when I was young watching my dad cross his cheque book stubs, with his bank statement. I cannot remember the last time I wrote a cheque or received a paper statement from any financial institution.

The way we manage our money has fundamentally changed and with it our behaviour and controls over our money have changed too.

Unlike cash, which offers a tangible sense of money leaving our hands, digital transactions are often invisible and can lead to unintended spending habits. Teens in particular are at risk of overspending through online platforms, subscription services and in-app purchases, without considering the long-term consequences. In addition, companies use the naivety and inexperience of young people to their advantage, when drawing them into purchases.

To help your Teen thrive in this digital world, it is crucial to provide them with a solid understanding of how digital money works and the self-discipline to manage it effectively. This includes teaching them to track their digital spending, set realistic limits and to recognise when digital platforms are encouraging impulse buys through targeted ads, or easy 'buy now' options.

It is the digital platforms' (and shops in general) job, to encourage people to part with their cash. It is our job to be wise to buyer psychology and help our Teens not to part with their cash, simply because it was made easy for them to do so. Being mindful about how, where and when our Teens spend their money, is key to them making purchases they actually need and not simply lean into the 'want' as discussed in the last chapter.

To help teens manage their money well, in this digital landscape, it's essential to equip them with the knowledge of how to track their spending, set limits and recognise the subtle ways digital platforms encourage impulsive spending. Understanding the differences between debit, credit and digital wallets, along with learning how to budget for online purchases, can help teens navigate the new world of digital money with confidence and control.

A key theme in the previous chapter was being aware of the numbers in your bank account. This has always been important, but is even more important in a digital world, where all barriers to spending money have been removed and with them, our ability to take our time in making decisions on how we spend our money. That is, unless we consciously choose to take control.

How to help teens navigate digital money

Understanding the psychology behind digital money can help parents guide their Teens towards more responsible spending habits. Teaching teens to track their expenses, set budgets and be mindful of impulse buying is essential for managing digital money wisely. It's important for them to know that while digital transactions offer convenience and flexibility, they also require discipline and awareness.

By equipping teens with these tools, they can take control of their finances, avoid common pitfalls like overspending or accumulating debt and develop healthy financial habits that will benefit them in the future.

We have to remember that digital money will be all our Teens know. Being given cash for their birthday will just be the preserve of grandparents, most other receipts of money will happen digitally, via bank transfer or similar. So, our Teens are possibly more confident in dealing digitally with money than their parents are.

I know it took me a while to utilise banking apps on my phone or using my phone to make contactless payments. Whilst for my Teens, this has been the only way they have ever paid for anything, other than the occasional cash transaction.

However, this is why it is even more important to talk to your Teen about the psychology of buying, which was not an issue when we were growing up. Yes, there were TV ads and the like when we were younger, but this was nothing compared to how social media and online marketing is set to encourage teens to purchase things they don't need and possibly can't really afford.

The psychology of digital spending vs cash

Spending physical cash gives you a tangible sense of the money leaving your hands. This connection had the ability to make people more mindful of their spending. With digital money however that connection disappears.

I can remember my mum giving me the cash to hand

over when I went shopping with her as a young child and feeling slightly bereft that it was being taken from me. However, children today do not have that experience of money, they don't see their parents handing over cash when completing a transaction. They are more likely to see a card or phone being tapped, followed by the now familiar sounding beep… and there isn't a lot, if any connection emotionally to that. It is purely transactional; nothing physically being handed over and left with someone else. Just a beep and job done; the goods are yours.

What message is this giving to our children? What are they thinking is taking place in terms of that transaction? Are they becoming disconnected from what money represents and their relationship with it? After all, can you have a positive relationship with something you cannot see?

Whether you are tapping a card or phone, or making an online purchase, the act of spending feels less engaged, more abstract and less connected. There is no immediate sense of what you are 'losing' or 'giving away', which can lead to spending more without realising it.

For teens, this lack of visibility around money can be especially problematic and again why it is so important to encourage them to actively and regularly engage with their numbers. Growing up in a digital-first environment, they're used to money as something invisible and therefore possibly unlimited. This opens up a situation where they unintentionally get into trouble because it is harder for them to gauge the impact of their financial decisions.

Remember, 'in-game purchases' and 'buy-now' bonuses, can leave teens wide open to spending money they really can't afford to spend. And at what cost? This is why it is important to talk to your Teens about how the digital financial world works and why it is their responsibility to be aware of how they are potentially being manipulated. Also how to avoid this damaging the future they want for themselves.

In a world of online selling and impulse buying – budgeting is your Teen's friend

I make no apology for labouring the point, of how

budgeting can be a mechanism to help your Teen overcome all of the coercive techniques and manipulation that want to help them part with their money. With a few clicks you can purchase anything and have it delivered to your doorstep within days and sometimes even minutes (one online shop promises to deliver your online shopping within 20 minutes if you live in a central location).

Online stores make it easier by storing your payment details, offering 'buy now pay later' options and targeting ads based on your browsing history. How brilliant for sellers… how dangerous for our Teens. This environment can make it difficult for teens to resist the temptation to spend, particularly when it comes without the emotional tie of actually handing cash over.

However, creating a budget and being emotionally connected to a goal that is important to you, can cause you to stop and think. Is this purchase a want or a need? If I purchase it, what impact will this have in the here and now and on achieving the goal I set for my budget? What if I delayed making this decision for 24 hours?

What if I decided to not make that purchase at all?

Encouraging your Teen to think in this way, is supporting them to be mindful of their purchase process and to take responsibility for that decision. This is empowerment. This is allowing them to consider the cost of their action and to understand the implication as well.

This is a way of really connecting them to their goals, and their money to those goals. It's making spending money personal and emotional. This beats the online providers at their own game.

Budgeting not only builds financial awareness, but it also strengthens the connection between your Teen, their money and their goals. When teens have a goal they care about, they are more likely to defend it from the impulsive temptations of online shopping. It's about equipping them to beat online providers at their own game by making conscious, goal-oriented choices that benefit their future and not the online seller's bottom line.

In a world full of distractions and endless digital

purchases, budgeting is more than just a financial tool, it's a way to help your Teen take control of their financial future and make thoughtful decisions that align with their long-term aspirations.

The darker side of online purchases

Talking to your Teen about money is not just about how to help them to better manage their money. It is also about making them aware of the increasing risk of scams and scammers, who are intent on not only taking your Teen's money, but stealing their financial identity, so they can use it to further line their pockets, at the cost of your Teen.

Yes, the convenience of online shopping has transformed the way we spend, it has also brought a more sinister element that both you and your Teen must be aware of. As we increasingly rely on digital platforms to make purchases, we expose our personal and financial information to potential cybercriminals. Teaching your Teen how to recognise and avoid these risks is essential for safeguarding their financial future.

When either you or your family are making online transactions, security should always be the first priority. Ensuring the websites and payment plan platforms you access are secure and encrypted all play an important role in keeping both your personal and financial details safe from scammers and hackers.

Scammers are getting far more sophisticated, and it is more difficult to spot scams than it used to be a few years ago. So, it is vital you ensure both yourself and your Teen are aware of all the ways you can protect yourself from becoming a victim of a scam.

There are many ways to do this including the following:

- When using a website look for https:// at the start of the URL as the 's' indicates that the website has a security certificate and is using encryption to protect your data.
- Encourage your Teen to only use trusted payment platforms such as PayPal, Apple Pay or Google. These platforms are vigilant when it comes to providing an extra layer of security

and act as a middleman between your bank and the vendor.

However, it is important to not be complacent and to assume that any payment platform is infallible. It is important to always be on your guard and advise your Teen to do the same. If you or they receive any message that is unexpected or questionable as far as its origin is concerned, stop and think, is this likely to be genuine or a scam?

Unfortunately, the Internet has become a hunting ground for scammers, and they will target either younger or older people because they may be less experienced in spotting red flags or questioning what is presented to them. Phishing activity is significantly on the increase and occurs when a scammer attempts to trick somebody into giving away personal data by pretending to be from a trusted company.

Fortunately, there are a number of ways you can spot a phishing scam and these include:

- **Unfamiliar email addresses** – Emails claiming to be from a trusted company may look and feel like they are legitimately from that company using their logo and branding. They often contain partial personal information but will have a link contained within the email and ask the recipient to click on the link, to confirm further personal details.

The easiest way to check if the e-mail is legitimate is to hover your mouse over the email address, as this will show the email address used to send the email from. If you have received previous emails from this company that you know are legitimate you can compare the previous and the current e-mail address for confirmation. However, the easiest thing to do if you are not certain is to find a telephone number from a trusted source and ring the company in question. **Do not click** on any link as banks and financial institutions will not be asking you to reveal any personal data by clicking a link. This is likely to be a phishing attempt, delete the email and report to the company it is purporting to be from.

- **Urgency or threat** - Phishing messages will try to create a sense of urgency claiming that something bad will happen if immediate action is not taken such as 'your account will be suspended unless you click here'. This is a significant red flag as reputable companies don't operate this way. **Do not click** on the link and report to the legitimate company.
- **Request for personal information** - Talk to your Teen about any requests for sensitive information they may receive. Make them aware that no legitimate business will ask for sensitive/private information such as passwords, credit card details etc. via e-mail or text.

Identity theft is also becoming much more widespread and the cost to victims ever increasing. However, there are a number of practical ways you and your Teen can protect yourselves, your information and your money.

- **Use strong passwords** - A strong password is your first line of defence. I know it can be a pain having to manage several unique passwords, but believe you me, having to unravel your accounts if your information ever gets stolen, that is a whole different level of pain and potential cost too. Passwords need to be strong, including a mix of letters, numbers and symbols and it's important to not replicate a password across multiple sites, use birthdates, or easy to remember words. Use an app like LastPass, that allows you to easily manage and update passwords.

- **Enable two-factor authentication (2FA)** - Two factor authentication adds an additional layer of security by requiring a second form of verification such as sending a code to your mobile, before accessing an account. Even if a hacker manages to get hold of a password, two-factor authentication can block unauthorised access.

- **Avoid public Wi-Fi for payment transactions** - Whilst it may appear attractive to log onto a public Wi-Fi network often these networks are unsecured, which makes it very easy for hackers to intercept your personal information. Ensure your Teen is made aware that sensitive transactions like banking or online shopping should never be done over a public Wi-Fi connection and should only be done on a secure private network. The mobile data network has additional levels of security, so if making a sensitive transaction whilst away from private home Wi-Fi, the mobile data network should be the network of choice.

What to do if financial information is compromised.

Despite taking all the recommended precautions, it is not always possible to protect your information. Things can sometimes go wrong. If your or your Teen's personal financial information is accessed, acting quickly can help to limit the damage.

- Firstly, notify your bank, credit card company or financial institution if there are suspicious transactions that you do not recognise and ask them to immediately freeze the relevant account and reverse any unauthorised charges.

- Change the password right away in the event of any breach. This applies to all accounts that could potentially be affected especially those linked to any financial institution you have accounts with.

- Set up an account with one of the credit agencies, as this will allow you to spot any anomalies easily and to have your accounts monitored for any signs of unusual activity. It is vital to keep an eye on bank statements and if you or your Teen spot anything you are not sure of, then contact the relevant financial institution right away. The earlier fraud is spotted, the easier it is going to be to contain it.

- If you or your Teen become the victim of identity theft, then it is important to report this to the relevant authorities. In the UK, an agency like Action Fraud, or in the US the Federal Trade Commission, will guide you through the recovery process and help you to prevent further damage.

Empowering your Teen to protect themselves.

Talking to your Teen about money includes ensuring they are aware about how to protect themselves from financial risk in the digital world. As your Teen becomes more independent with their money it is vital they know how to recognise scams, secure their accounts and prevent their personal information from falling into the wrong hands. This will ensure they know how to navigate the online space both confidently and safely.

By equipping your Teen with all these relevant tools, you are not only helping them to avoid costly mistakes but also instilling lifelong habits of financial caution and responsibility that will serve them both now and in the future. This awareness is just as important as knowing how to manage their money well. It's about protecting their financial future in a world that is both increasingly digital and at times more dangerous.

Exercise

Online Spending Awareness Tracker

Objective: Help your Teen become more aware of their online spending habits and triggers.

Instructions

1. **Track for a week** - Ask your Teen to note each time they think about or make an online purchase for one week. They should include -
    - What they wanted to buy.
    - Where they saw it (social media, ad, app, etc.).
    - How they felt in that moment (excited, bored, pressured).

2. **Reflect** - At the end of the week, review together -

- What types of things caught their attention most?
- How often did they feel tempted to buy without planning to?
- What patterns do they notice?

This exercise gives teen's insight into their online spending triggers, helping them understand and manage their habits better.

For an additional layer of discussion, you do the exercise at the same time, so you have a shared experience and shared learning with your Teen.

BUT REMEMBER, THIS IS A JUDGEMENT FREE SPACE. THE PURPOSE OF THIS EXERCISE IS TO EDUCATE YOUR TEEN AND NOT TO TELL THEM OFF.

Notes

CHAPTER 8
UNDERSTANDING CREDIT AND AVOIDING DEBT

The first thing to say about this chapter, is that if your Teen is under 18 right now, this information will not be relevant to him or her, as you are unable to take out credit or debt, until you are over the age of 18. However, the sooner you educate them on the importance of what credit and debt is and how to manage it responsibly, the less likely it will cause them any problems later in life. So no matter how old they are, start to have these conversations now.

I have already shared my experience of credit cards and debt as a teen, due to my naivety and lack of real awareness about how cleverly credit card companies market their products to inexperienced young people. I was bombarded with attractive offers that simply encouraged me to get into debt at a time when easy money was too attractive to say no to.

Fortunately for me, whilst there was a financial cost in terms of the high interest rates that credit card companies charge on an annual basis, I was still able to maintain those payments. Once the penny did drop, I was working full-time and happily in a position to pay off the balance quickly. However, the same cannot be said for all teens or even adults, because credit card companies are very good at promoting their services and unless we really know how to fully understand the cost, we can get caught out and take out debt that we simply can't afford.

Essentially although perceived differently, credit and debt are two sides of the same financial coin, influencing every big decision we make in our lives, from buying a car or a house, to managing daily expenses. It is therefore vital that your Teen understands how credit and debt work and how it can impact their financial stability.

However, while debt can sometimes be painted as bad and to be avoided, it's not as simple as that. When managed well, debt can be a foundation for financial growth, opening doors to investment opportunities and experiences.

Credit is borrowed money that must be repaid over time, usually with added interest, which can be at extremely high rates. However, when used wisely credit can be a helpful tool for achieving long-term goals. For example, taking out a loan for education or a small business can be a positive step towards building a future.

However, just like I have encouraged you to have the conversation with your Teen about mindful spending, it is also important to be mindful about your own use and your Teen's use of credit and debt as well. If I use my own experience as an example, I was simply living beyond my means, funding my student lifestyle via a credit card. That was not sensible, mindful or the purpose for which credit or debt should ever be used, because of the high cost attached to it.

As a parent we should always encourage our children to live within their means and if necessary, find ways to boost their income and not to take out costly debt that could cause problems further down the line.

Whilst the right kind of debt can be a good thing, this is something that should come much later for your Teen. Right now, they need to establish the right relationship with money and understand both the upside and downside of credit cards, bank loans and other forms of credit. If they don't learn about this now, they are leaving themselves wide open to high interest rates, potentially struggling to pay down what they owe and falling into a cycle of debt, which they may fail to get out of.

This type of debt can create significant financial strain, which can impact not only your Teen's future spending power but their long-term financial health.

It is important that your Teen has the information they need to make the right decisions about credit and debt and that they are not simply drawn into utilising it based on clever and creative marketing techniques.

By understanding the difference between good and bad debt and learning to manage credit responsibly, your Teen will start to build healthy financial habits that lead to stability, security and opportunities in the future. Something all parents want for their children, right?

The fundamentals of credit

Is it my parents' fault that I had very little awareness about credit cards and the danger of living beyond my means when I was a teen? Absolutely not, back then we spoke very little about money, it was even more of an off-limits topic than it is today.

However, we know the pitfalls now of what happens when we don't have open conversations with our children about money. As the poet Maya Angelou said, "When we know better, we must do better" and now is the time to do better. And how do we do better? By talking about how money works and more importantly how our Teens can make it work for them and this includes understanding what credit actually is.
Credit is simply the ability to borrow money, with the promise of paying it back later. Usually with a lot of

added interest. In practical terms when you use credit, such as a credit card or loan, you're borrowing funds from a lender, like a bank or credit card company, with the understanding that you will repay them over time. How much you repay and how long you have to repay, depends on the credit terms, which include the interest rate and over what length of time.

Credit scores – why you need to understand them

Something else related to credit that I had no awareness of when I signed up for my first credit card, was a credit score and how this can impact your financial health and future. A credit score is a three-digit number that reflects your credit worthiness or how trustworthy you are in the opinion of lenders. Credit scores typically range from 300 to 999 with higher scores indicating better creditworthiness. Your credit score is calculated based on several factors which include:

- Payment history - do you make payments on time?

- Credit utilisation - how much of your available credit are you using?
- Length of credit history - how long have you been using credit?
- Types of credit - do you have a mix of credit types e.g., credit cards, loans etc.?
- New credit application inquiries - how often are you applying for new credit?

It is worth noting that you will not have a credit score until you are over the age of 18, as credit is not allowed until you are legally an adult.

However, it's important that you make your Teen aware of the impact their credit history can have on their future financial health. Each of these elements above, determine an individual's credit score and a higher credit score can open doors to better long-term loans and lower interest rates saving them money in the future. For example, a person with a high score may get a car loan with a lower interest rate, while someone with a lower score may face higher costs for the same loan. This is because finance companies base their interest rates on their belief of the risk to them in providing credit to an individual.

Credit reports detail your credit history, including any loans, credit cards and payment records. These reports are compiled by credit bureaux such as Experian, Equifax and Trans Union and they provide a detailed picture of how a person has managed their debt. Each time you borrow money or make a payment, this activity is reported to the credit agency and used to update your credit report.

Lenders use credit reports to assess the risk of lending money to you. A positive credit report with a high score demonstrates responsible borrowing and timely payments which can increase your chances of being approved for credit.

However, be aware that a report showing missing payments or high levels of debt can make lenders cautious, resulting in higher interest rates or even refusal to provide credit. All of which is included in your credit report and reflected in your credit score.

Whilst I was at university happily utilising my credit card, fortunately I was able to maintain my commitments to pay for the debt I was carrying. However I had no awareness of the rate of interest I was being charged, how that interest was being compounded i.e. the interest was being charged on the balance and the interest I accrued over time, so stealthily increasing without my active knowledge. Added to this, I was not aware of the impact it was probably having on my credit score.

I say having, due to the fact at this time I was blissfully ignorant about credit scores and reports. In fact, so blissfully unaware was I, I had long paid off that credit card balance once I became aware of how much it was actually costing me. By the time credit scores entered my awareness, I had seemingly managed to repair any damage, with ill-effect. But the story COULD have been very, very different.

Don't let your Teen be me. Don't let them remain ignorant, as managing money today is much harder as a student, than it was in my day. For a start, university education did not come with a cost to it, there were no tuition fees and there certainly weren't student loans. When I left university, I was overdrawn by less than £500, due to my strong work ethic, but also to not living through a cost-of-living crisis at that the same time!

This is why now, in a very different world financially, with so many easy ways to influence a teen's buying behaviour, it is vital they understand the fundamentals; of credit scores, credit reports and how credit works, this will allow them to make informed choices and build a healthy financial future.

Managing credit well isn't just about borrowing money, it's also about creating opportunities and maintaining financial flexibility as you grow.

What if as a parent, you have not been good at managing credit yourself?

It is possible that right now you are asking yourself, "How can I talk to my Teen about not getting into debt and utilising credit effectively, when I have not managed this for myself?" It may be you have a poor credit rating and/or far too much debt. Please don't let this stop you from talking to your Teen about this hugely important subject, because of the way you feel about your circumstances.

It is likely there are good reasons why you are in the situation you are. You might have been like me and not known any better when you were younger. Or circumstances have meant you needed to rely on debt and credit cards, much more than you would have liked. However do you want history to repeat itself? I know the answer is no.

This is why you have purchased this book. This is why you have started to talk to your Teen about money, because you don't want them to have the same lived experience as you.

This is not about your experience (although I can help you with this too), this is about ensuring history does not repeat itself for your Teen. I will repeat again, 'when you know better, you do better'.

Please remember sharing your own experiences, even

the struggles, can be one of the most powerful ways to support your Teen. By being honest about your own challenges with credit, you can offer them real life insight into what to avoid and the importance of building good money, right at the start of their relationship with it.

You don't need a perfect credit history yourself to effectively guide your Teen, in fact honestly sharing your experience can serve as the best and most valuable lesson for them.

You might begin the conversation by acknowledging managing credit is not easy and using this as a conversation starter, to share what you have learnt from your own experience. Let me also say, this is not about feeling shame or hiding your own past mistakes, it's about providing relevant context, to empower your Teen to make smarter decisions.

You could begin the conversation by saying, "I learnt the hard way and I want to help you avoid the same mistakes by providing you with a real-life example, that I hope will resonate more than any lecture could."

This is taking your experience and using it to help create a different future for your Teen. A great reframe, in terms of it 'happened for you, not to you', so you were able to share that experience with your child.

This is not about you focusing on what hasn't gone well, rather it's about what you want for your Teen's future. By talking openly to them about money, you are providing them with the awareness that will help them to make confident decisions around credit, allowing them to avoid the same pitfalls. After all the conversations you are now having with them about money, it is as much about their financial futures, as it is about the confidence you're building together as a family.

Building healthy credit habits

A mistake made by many adults is, they actually avoid having credit or debt at all. Having no debt or credit, means that you have no credit score or report for a financial institution to base a credit decision on and therefore it is unlikely you will be able to obtain credit in the future.

Why is this important to know? Without demonstrating you can manage credit well, you are likely to find it difficult to obtain credit for a significant life purchase, like a mortgage, bank loan or other larger purchase that you can't afford to pay for with cash.

I have known many people who were fearful of credit and saw it as a negative thing, not understanding why they were turned down for credit when eventually they decided they wanted to apply for it. This is because the bank, credit card company etc., had no evidence on which to judge the individual's credit worthiness and therefore turned them down.

This initially may not make any sense, but just because you don't have any formal debt, this is not automatically a sign that you are brilliant at managing your money. You might have a high amount of informal debt, such as borrowing from friends or the 'Bank of Mum and Dad', so without evidence to make their decision on, financial institutions will simply say no.

This is why creating and continuing to build healthy credit habits is vital for your Teen, in order for them to create the evidence that they are actually good at managing their money. Developing sound habits around borrowing, spending and repaying credit, will enable your Teen to avoid common debt traps and create a strong foundation for future financial goals.

Again, this element is only directly relevant to teens who have reached the age of 18, but the sooner you start having these conversations with your Teen, the sooner they will understand the benefits of building the right habits around managing their money and their credit.

There are ways that your Teen, once they are old enough to take out credit, can ensure they understand and use credit responsibly. Remember they need to build a strong and solid credit score, which is based on the information that goes into their credit report, so how do they do that?

Pay bills on time, every time

One of the most important habits to commit to and manage is paying all bills on time. Doing so demonstrates to lenders that you take your financial commitments seriously and that you are responsible and reliable. Late or missed payments can seriously affect a credit score, which can make it difficult to borrow money in the future and lead to higher rates of interest being charged.

Keep balances low

It's vital to avoid having a high balance on credit cards, as this can make it much harder to repay and quickly lead to debt that may be hard to manage. Ideally, you should encourage your Teen to only use a small percentage of their available credit each month. Ideally no more than 30%. For example, if a teen has a credit limit of £500, they should try to keep their balance under £150. The concept of 'credit utilisation' is a big factor in calculating credit scores.

Encourage your Teen to pay off the whole balance every month, by the due date of payment at the very latest. This way they demonstrate how well they are managing their money and that they are spending well within their means. It also means they don't pay any interest. Remember, the purpose of them having a credit card, is not to live beyond their means, but to build up a strong credit rating they can benefit from in the future.

Only borrow what they can afford

I know for me, back in my student days, credit felt like 'free money', but it was not. It's essential your Teen knows any money borrowed must be paid back AND usually with a high rate of interest. Teens should only borrow what they can afford to repay, in total, on time and within their budget. Encouraging this approach and mindset towards money early on, can help teens avoid debt, whilst developing good financial discipline.

As a parent remind them, if they can't afford to pay off the balance in full at the end of the month (before the interest is added), then it is better they don't make the purchase until such a time they can afford to pay the credit card balance off on time. This habit helps your Teen understand the difference between wants and needs, which in turn leads to more mindful spending.

Always read the small print

Remind your Teen that credit card companies and other financial institutions will have marketing departments whose job it is to make taking out one of their products very attractive to their would-be customers. It is the would-be customers' job to ensure they read the small print, to understand what they are signing up for. This includes understanding the interest rates, payment terms, fees and any payments for penalties. Now whilst I don't encourage any teen take a financial product when they feel it may be beyond their means, sometimes situations arise and things happen and it's important your Teen is aware of the risk and cost to signing up for a credit card etc. and does not enter into such an arrangement without being fully aware of the facts.

Encourage your Teen to ask questions if they are unsure about the terms and remind them that knowing all the details upfront can save money and worry later down the line.

Be clear about the financial commitment your Teen is taking on

No financial arrangement should ever be entered into lightly and if you don't believe your Teen is ready for that level of commitment at this stage, then encourage them to stay away from entering into such an arrangement and talk to them about the behaviours they need to be demonstrating in order to indicate they are now ready to take that next step.

This could be by setting a personal spending limit each week/month that aligns with their income or allowance. By setting limits, they are demonstrating they are actively practicing self-discipline and are able to manage their finances without over-extending themselves. Openly discussing with them, that taking out a credit card is not for the purpose of having access to more money. It is for the purpose of building a positive credit report and from there a strong credit score. If they cannot afford to repay the balance in full, then they should stay clear of taking out credit.

Before your Teen commits to taking out credit, encourage them to keep a record of what they spend, in one of the suggested ways discussed in Chapter Three within this book. This way they will get a clear picture of where their money goes and can adjust, creating healthy habits before they take on credit.

Building financial confidence for the future

By actively supporting your Teen to develop healthy habits early, you are helping them to create a positive relationship not only with money but also with credit. By committing to paying bills on time, paying off the balance each month, borrowing within their means, understanding credit terms and setting spending limits, they are setting themselves up to navigate both their money and credit responsibly.

These habits will not only help them to avoid developing an unhealthy relationship with money and credit but develop the discipline to make confident and informed financial decisions that align with their long-term goals. How powerful is that?

❛Let's Talk!❜

Exercise – Wants vs Needs

Objective

To support your Teens to think critically before using credit, it is worthwhile asking them to explore if the purchase is a want or a need.

Step 1.

Ask your Teen to pick three items they would like to buy right now and to write them down. These could be anything; clothing, gadgets, tickets to a gig or even something bigger like a car.

Step 2.

Ask your Teen to categorise each item, as either a need (they absolutely have to have it, it is essential) or a want (something that is not essential but would be nice to have).

Step 3.

Ask your Teen to consider, if it were possible, would they use a credit card to buy each item. If yes - why? If not - why not?

Have a short discussion with your Teen on how easy it can be to justify spending on wants (as opposed to needs) and how easy it could be to fall into a bad habit or using credit to fund unnecessary purchases....and what the additional costs might be.

_____

_____

_____

_____

_____

_____

_____

_____

CHAPTER 9

HOW TO HAVE DIFFICULT CONVERSATIONS ABOUT MONEY

Let's face it, talking about money is still something many adults find uncomfortable, so if those who are well beyond their teenage years find it uncomfortable, how on earth can we expect Teens to find it a comfortable conversation? Especially if, up until now, you as their parent(s) haven't openly spoken about money.

We know there is still a huge taboo around talking about money. Be honest, you would prefer to share your favourite sex position with your friends than have a conversation about money! Yes, I know this is funny, but it is also serious. If you can't talk about money, then it is unlikely your Teen can, and this can get them into serious trouble.

Money is still treated as a secretive topic, that 'nice' people don't talk about. This attitude can make it hard for adults and teens to bring it up naturally in conversation. The fact that many would rather talk about anything other than money, shows just how deep this discomfort is.

When money is not talked about openly, this can lead teens to believe it is something secretive or even shameful. This can lead them to feel uncertain or embarrassed, fearing it is a topic that is off limits because it is not being talked about at home, creating a vicious circle.

If teens have not been encouraged to talk openly about money as they are growing up, what then happens when they need to have difficult conversations about money? What happens…often nothing happens and whatever the problem is, it tends to become bigger, because the teen has not been able to address it.

So, let's start by identifying the kinds of difficult

conversations about money, you need to have with your Teen. Below I suggest ways you as a parent can open up these conversations:

- **Discussing money with friends** – Teens often feel peer pressure to keep up with their friends' spending habits, such as latest fashion trends, gadgets, or days/nights out. Admitting a lack of funds can feel embarrassing, shameful or awkward and can lead to fear of being judged or excluded from the friendship group.

  Parent talk - If this situation is relevant, it would be useful if your Teen could have a conversation with their friends as to why they can't afford to do something or to buy a particular item and to discuss alternatives that fit their budget. It could be the friends are also relieved that they don't have to try and 'fit in' or live up to certain expectations.

- **Asking for financial support from parents** – Teens may feel embarrassed or reluctant to ask for money, particularly if they feel they should be 'old enough' to manage on their own. There may also be a concern that in asking for support, they are putting pressure on their parents, disappointing their parents, or be worried they will be seen as irresponsible.

Parent talk – In this situation encourage your Teen to talk about what additional support they might need, for things like school activities, hobbies, or unexpected expenses. Let them know that you appreciate they are still learning about how to manage their money and that where you can, you want to help and at least be a sounding board on how to support them to find the right solution.

- **Setting strong boundaries around lending money to friends** – This can be a tricky situation for teens to experience. Teens can find it extremely uncomfortable to say no to a friend, even when they don't have the money to lend. They may worry about the effect saying no will have on the friendship or coming across as 'tight'.

Parent talk – Explain to your Teen, ideally before it has even happened, that they can and must politely decline a friend's request to borrow money, by explaining that in the long term, this will protect the friendship, as well as protecting their own finances. Encourage your Teen to come and speak to you should this situation arise, as this will provide your Teen with the confidence they can talk to you.

- **Talking about part-time jobs and income expectations** - For some teens deciding whether to take on a part time job and balancing this with education responsibilities can be difficult. Teens may also feel they lack experience on negotiating wages, working hours, or discussing job responsibilities. As teens move towards becoming young adults, they may feel they should be more independent than their age would realistically suggest.

Parent talk - As a parent encourage your Teen to talk about having a part-time job. Explain to them the positive aspects of having more independence, as well as more money. However, balance this with any concerns you or they may have about impact on their school studies or other commitments. Again, it is ideal to have this conversation before it becomes an issue, but equally just having the conversation will provide your Teen with the knowledge that they can openly talk to you about their ambitions and concerns without fear of judgement.

- **Managing peer pressure and social media -** Teens are likely to be influenced by many more marketing touch points then we as parents experienced at that age. Social media pervades so much of our Teen's lives, which can lead to pressure to spend money on particular brands, going to certain events or taking part in particular experiences. Add to this peer pressure from friends, which can lead to teens feeling left out, self-conscious and even questioning their own self-worth.

Parent talk - Have an open conversation with your Teen, about how social media works and how marketing is designed to create a real sense of FOMO (fear of missing out). This is an ideal opportunity to talk to your Teen about their financial goals and budget and help them to work out prioritising those goals over a particular spending trend. It also provides the opportunity to discuss with your Teen that if there is really something they want to buy or to experience what they can do to create the funds. This encourages them to become resourceful and to further understand the importance of delayed gratification.

- **Navigating family money conversations and boundaries** - This can be an extremely difficult topic as teens may become aware of money struggles or changes within the family finances, leading to anxiety, fear or guilt. Talking to their parents about these issues can be scary, or intimidating, especially if they have concerns about overstepping boundaries or causing their parents distress.

Parent talk - It is really important to be honest and as upfront with your Teen as possible if family financial circumstances change. Our children are extremely intuitive and dialled in to the household dynamics. It is important that you are able to provide them with reassurance if they start to ask questions, without them feeling like they are prying into adult money matters.

It may arise, if they are working, that they want to discuss ways they can contribute or help. If this situation happens, it is an ideal opportunity to demonstrate that you respect their input and recognise they may have an alternative view that could help improve the situation. Under no circumstances allow your Teen to take on any blame for the current financial situation the family is in. Reassure them that you are the adult and will be responsible for resolving the issue.

- **Talking about money related concerns around education and hobbies** - As teens start to plan for university or other post school experiences, they may feel concern in talking to their parents about what financial support may be available. They may also need to discuss the cost of their extracurricular activities in order to help them prioritise additional costs.

Parent talk - It is useful to start having conversations with your Teen as soon as possible about budgeting for future goals and potential costs, so next steps can be clearly identified and agreed. It would be useful to research together what student loans are available for tuition fees and maintenance allowances and what additional support might be available through bursaries and grants.

This is the ideal opportunity for you to make your Teen aware of what financial support you may or may not be able to offer, making it clear to them you will support them to find a way to achieve their next step goal. During these kinds of conversations, it isn't always about finding the exact solution immediately but having an open dialogue with regards to what might be possible. This supports your Teen in developing their own resourcefulness and gently encourages them to become more independent in a way they don't feel they have to do it all by themselves.

- **Talking about debt (including student loans)** - It's important to remember that money is largely not discussed in school in any meaningful way and unless you have had a conversation with your Teen on a regular basis about credit and debt it is unlikely they will be familiar with the topic. Conversations about debt or establishing credit can feel confusing, overwhelming and a topic to be avoided at all costs.

However, as a parent, if up until now you haven't spoken to your Teen about these hugely important areas of money, now is the ideal opportunity to do so.

Parent talk - Take the opportunity to talk openly to your Teen about credit cards, loans and responsible debt management so they have the opportunity to understand both the benefits and risks involved and ask questions in a safe, judgement-free way. I have shared in this book my first experience of having a credit card and I have also shared this with my own Teens, as an example of how credit card companies draw you in with talk of easy money. I have put myself forward as an example of how not to use credit. If you have a similar (or a different example), where you can share from the scar and not the wound (in other words, you are not going through a stressful financial situation right now, that might cause more distress than the lesson it teaches), this is an ideal opportunity to share this with your Teen.

- **Becoming financially independent** - This can be tricky to navigate for both parents and teens. As teens grow, they are likely to want more control over their money, which can lead to arguments with parents who are used to managing money on the children's behalf. The challenge lies in discovering a balance that works for everyone.

Parent talk - As difficult as it can be to accept in practise, our role as a parent is to help to support our children so they no longer need us. This also applies to money. As parents, it is essential we raise our children to become emotionally and financially independent. The best way to do this is to discuss boundaries around how much you as a parent should control your Teen's spending and saving, whilst at the same time supporting them to make good decisions around money. This does not have to be an 'all or nothing' approach and it is important that your Teen understands that with money comes responsibility. How you do this in practise should be discussed with your Teen based on how old they are. The older they are, the more independence you should start to offer them.

- **Dealing with money mistakes and taking responsibility** - Admitting to financial mistakes, like overspending, forgetting to pay a bill on time, or breaking a budget, can be difficult for adults and teens. This is because we all want to appear responsible. But there is an added layer of emotional complexity a teen may have to deal with, including feeling they have let their parents down, fear of being a disappointment or generating consequences the parents may have to deal with.

Parent talk - As parents and adults we know owning up to a financial mistake is the best way to deal with it. It allows us to ask for guidance and in doing so avoid repeating the same mistake. Having an open and honest conversation with your Teen about avoiding financial mistakes in the first place is the ideal scenario, however we also know whilst learning any new skill, mistakes will happen. So let your Teen know they can talk to you and you will do your best to come up with a suitable solution.

- **Planning for large purchases** - Remember when you were a teen, I bet you had big financial goals that didn't necessarily match with the family budget or priorities. I am going to hazard a guess the same is true of your Teen today and this can create tension, especially if they want to spend a lot of money on an item that may not seem essential to parents.

Parent talk - It is important to remember that as we get older our values and what is most important to us change. It is also useful to reflect back to what used to be important to us when we were younger. If and when this situation arises with your Teen, this is the ideal opportunity for you to model the right behaviour. Let them discuss why a particular purchase is important to them. Help them to create a savings plan and discuss any support they might need from the family. This is the perfect opportunity for you to understand your Teen's value system currently and show them they can talk to you. Even if you don't agree with their goals at that point in time. Remember this all links back to their need for financial independence, but you can also link it to helping them understand responsible decision-making when it comes to money.

- **Preparing for financial independence and life post school** - Planning those next steps post school can involve serious financial considerations regarding the costs involved. If considering university, teens may find it overwhelming to discuss the level of support they can expect and what they and you will be responsible for. The media talks about the cost involved in obtaining a university degree in such a way that some teens might feel is unattainable for them. Whilst they would like to further their education, the pressure of the money involved could lead them to simply dismiss it, as not being possible for them. This could lead to them missing out on an opportunity, before they have even really considered it.

Parent talk - As parents we know how quickly time flies, from when our children are babies, to suddenly being fully grown adults! This can mean we miss the opportunity to understand what their ambitions are. So, I would encourage you to have this conversation as soon as possible so you and they can talk about what their goals are once they leave school. This will ensure they have all the facts and figures with regards to the opportunity cost and if and how you can support them. Today, going to university is not the only way to achieve a degree. There are more and more companies now offering degree-level apprenticeships, which provide employees with the ability to earn and learn while achieving a degree. This not only avoids the cost of studying for a degree but also provides the young person with the opportunity to gain direct work experience, earn money and have a job at the end of the process. So, the sooner you start talking to your Teen about their personal aspirations, the sooner you can support them to develop a plan that is right for them.

We have looked at the areas where our Teens are likely to find talking about money difficult, now let's look at the blueprint for how we can ensure those conversations are not only had but are as comfortable as possible.

Start by ensuring you are encouraging open discussions at home. Simply by reading this book you have shown your commitment to wanting to not only talk to your Teen about money, but to helping them to initiate those conversations as well. It is important to model transparency and the best way to do this is to have open conversations about your own financial decisions, challenges and goals.

This is not about you revealing anything you feel will be too exposing or indeed worrying for your Teen, it is about opening up a conversation where you and they can move forward positively. For example, talking about budgeting, saving, or why you prioritise certain expenses. This demonstrates to your Teen that money does not have to be a secret or an uncomfortable topic.

By you normalising the money conversation, you will be demonstrating to your Teen that talking about money is a healthy, important and necessary part of life. This can be introduced very early on, for example, casually bringing up everyday decisions like grocery budgeting or savings goals to show that money discussions don't have to be limited to negative or stressful conversations.

It is important to explain to your Teen the value of having difficult conversations around money. Do this by explaining that setting boundaries with others may help them to make better and more informed decisions. For example, you could say to your Teen that talking about money can help them to achieve their financial goals and to ensure others understand their priorities.

It is important that you remind your Teen that developing personal boundaries not just around money, will serve them throughout their lives. By learning to clearly communicate about money now, they will be better prepared to handle and manage bigger financial conversations when they are older, from negotiating salaries to discussing financial priorities with a partner.

It is also important to explain that everyone has their own unique relationship with money that has been influenced by their background, experiences and values. It will help your Teen to understand that it is important to approach conversations about money with curiosity and empathy. For example, if a friend or family member sees money differently from them that's ok.

Understanding their perspective can make the conversation easier.

It is also important to encourage your Teen to focus on listening without interrupting or assuming, however it is important that you model the same behaviour yourself around your Teen. This helps your Teen see that you respect their views and opinions and are prepared to give them space to share them.

Something my clients find very useful when having difficult conversations about money is the use of 'I' statements. 'I' statements are helpful in allowing individuals to express their thoughts without sounding accusatory or defensive. For example, rather than 'you shouldn't expect me to pay for you', instead consider saying 'I feel more comfortable if we each cover our own expenses'.

It is useful to practise scenarios where you and your Teen can use, 'I' statements in a safe way. You could role-play a situation where a friend asks your Teen for money and they respond with something like, 'I'm currently saving for something important so unfortunately, I'm not able to lend you any money. This can provide your Teen with the confidence to address a live situation when, or if, it occurs and to have the answer readily available. It can help them move forward positively without concern around any repercussions.

The use of 'I' statements and role-playing can also be taken a step further, where you give your Teen some sample answers to common money scenarios, such as setting a spending limit, going out with friends or asking for financial support. For example: 'I'd like to split the bill so I can stay within my budget.'

You can help your Teen brainstorm responses that offer them alternatives, like suggesting an affordable activity if a friend suggests an expensive one. I'm sure we can all recall situations when we were put on the spot or unprepared and subsequently responded in a way we would not have done had we been better prepared. This will also encourage your Teen to come and talk to you more openly about their concerns or actively ask your advice about a particular situation.

It is however also important to make your Teen aware

that money conversations often involve compromise. Teens should also be made aware that they are unlikely to get the exact outcome they want in a conversation around money, but by being open and prepared to compromise this will prepare them for similar situations in the future.

It is always a good practice to encourage your Teen to self-reflect after each challenging conversation. This will encourage them to reflect on what they felt worked well and what they might do differently should the situation arise again. You could ask them what part of the conversation felt comfortable, was there anything that was harder than expected. Doing this self-reflection, will encourage your Teen to take responsibility for the outcome of that conversation and be more mindful about it.

It is also an important part of the process to help your Teen to celebrate small wins, as this will help to build their confidence by recognising their efforts, regardless of the outcome of the conversation. Learning to have difficult conversations is a skill and it is something that needs to be practiced.

By you guiding your Teen through these steps, you're giving them the tools to approach all money conversations with confidence, empathy and clear communication. For most, these skills don't come naturally, however these skills will empower your Teen to handle conversations around money with family, friends or anyone else as they grow. It is a skill for life that they will eventually thank you for helping them develop.

Let's Talk!

Exercise

Role-Reversal Money Conversation
Objective - quickly build empathy and practise discussing a difficult money topic with clarity and understanding.

Step 1. Choose a Money Topic (1 minute)
- Select a simple topic, like asking for more pocket money/a bigger allowance, budgeting for

a day out with friends, or saying no to lending money.

Step 2. Switch Roles (1 minute)

- The parent acts as the teen and makes a request, such as, "I'd like more pocket money/a bigger allowance for weekends."
- The teen takes on the parent role and responds briefly with their thoughts or concerns.

Step 3. Practice "I" Statements and Listening (2 minutes)

- The 'teen' explains why they want the change, starting with "I" statements (e.g., "I feel I need more because…").
- The 'parent' listens, summarises briefly and responds. Aim for two exchanges only to keep it short and focused.

Step 4. Reflect Together (2 minutes)

- Switch back to your original roles and discuss.
    - "What did you understand about my perspective?"
    - "What's one thing we could both remember for future conversations?"

This exercise quickly builds understanding in just a few minutes, while giving both parent and teen a chance to practice discussing money clearly and respectfully.

_____

_____

_____

_____

_____

_____

_____

_____

_____

CHAPTER 10
HELPING YOUR TEEN STAY SAFE ONLINE

So much of our lives is now managed online and this also includes our money. This is why it is so important we ensure our Teens are educated on how to stay safe online. This includes how to recognise a scam and how to protect their financial identity, to ensure they do not become victim to one of the many scams that continuously try to trap us.

Scammers have become very sophisticated at convincing their victims to inadvertently provide them with access to personal information and bank account details. This can result in not only financial loss to the victim, but also their financial identity being fraudulently used for further gain by the scammer.

Scammers are targeting those who are less experienced and more naive. Teens are amongst the largest demographic falling victim to the many scams that are happening and evolving all the time.

Part of the problem is online interactions are a big part of daily life for teens, from social media to online shopping. Recent research has shown that young people are the most likely to fall victim to a scam purely down to the fact that they access online services more frequently than other segments of the population. It is therefore really important as parents that we emphasise the importance of staying informed and vigilant to avoid risks like fraud, identity theft and inappropriate content.

If you are not doing so already, start having these conversations with your Teen. Provide them with real-life, relatable examples, such as a friend who had their account hacked or experienced online bullying, to highlight the need for awareness.

You could say something like, 'In today's world so much of what we do, from chatting with friends, to making purchases is done online. But please remember with this convenience also comes responsibility. Just as I know you want to protect your personal space in real life, it's equally important to protect your space online too.'

We must remember our Teens tend to think they are invincible and are always right! Despite knowing most people learn from experience, becoming the victim of fraud or having to deal with the fallout of having your financial identity stolen is an experience I would suggest everybody wants to avoid. Start the conversation by making your Teen aware of the types of risk they could be exposed to.

Breakdown common online threats including scams, hacking, identity theft, phishing and cyberbullying. You may not know very much about any of these directly yourself. I hope you don't! So let me break each area down for you, so that you can discuss this more confidently with your Teen.

Scams

A scam is a scheme designed to dishonestly trick people into giving away their personal information, money or valuables. Scammers often use fake promises, urgent messages, or 'too good to be true offers' to lure their targets, creating a sense of trust or urgency to get what they want. Scams can appear as emails, texts, phone calls, or social media messages and they're carefully crafted to look real, which makes them difficult to spot. Being aware of common scam tactics and staying cautious online, are key ways to avoid falling victim to these schemes.

Here's a recent example from our household of such a scam that is currently doing the rounds. One morning my teenage son excitedly declared on opening his e-mail, that he had won a big prize in a competition. However, he needed to fill out a form and provide credit card details to pay for the postage required for the prize to be sent to him. Fortunately, we have spoken frequently to our children about scams and how they should be vigilant online, so my son was already starting to become suspicious.

He said to me that he didn't believe this was real and that it was a scam, because he could not remember entering a competition with this company and was suspicious when they asked for personal details as well as a credit card number. When I looked at the e-mail and checked the e-mail address it was sent from, it was very clear it was a scam, and we deleted the e-mail straight away.

I often remind both my children, when something appears out of the blue, especially an unexpected 'win', I encourage them, as I do myself, to pause and ask two key questions:
1. Is it possible?
2. Is it probable?

These simple but effective questions can help filter out scams and 'too good to be true' offers, reinforcing the need to be sceptical and develop critical thinking, when making decisions involving money.

Hacking

Hacking is the process of gaining unauthorised access to someone else's computer, network, or personal accounts, usually with the intent to steal information, disrupt services, or cause harm. Hackers use various methods such as guessing weak passwords, exploiting software vulnerabilities, or tricking people into revealing personal details, through phishing scams (more on this shortly). While some hacking is done by individuals who intend to cause harm or steal data, others may do it to expose security weaknesses. Protecting accounts with strong, unique passwords and enabling additional security features, like 2-factor authentication (2FA), can prevent hacking attempts.

You must encourage your Teen to adopt as many security features as they can, such as avoiding using the same password across other accounts, to regularly change their passwords (see something like LastPass to manage passwords) and to stay vigilant when providing any personal information online.

Discourage them from providing any personal information, unless they are 100% convinced it is being asked for legitimately and advise them that no bank or financial institution will ask them to provide details like PINs, bank card details, etc. - ever.

Phishing

Phishing is a type of online scam where attackers pretend to be trusted sources like banks, popular websites or even friends. It has become a very common way for scammers to trick people into sharing personal information such as credit card numbers, passwords or other sensitive details. It used to be easy to spot a phishing e-mail, with poor spelling and grammar or the incorrect use of a company's logo and branding. However, over recent years, scams have become more and more sophisticated and more difficult to spot as a result.

Phishing attempts come in various forms; fake emails, text messages or social media links. They can look completely legitimate, but direct victims to fraudulent websites or prompt them to download harmful software. This then provides access to personal details directly from their victim's devices. Phishing messages typically create a sense of urgency or fear, which pressures people into responding quickly and not thinking logically. Being cautious about unexpected requests and verifying the source before clicking links or sharing information can help you and your Teen avoid phishing attacks.

Cyberbullying

Cyberbullying, as the name suggests, is a form of bullying. It takes place online, or through digital devices, such as smartphones, tablets and computers. Social media platforms have become an easy way for cyberbullies to target their victims, but messaging apps, online chatrooms and gaming communities are also commonly used to bully victims.

Unlike traditional bullying, cyberbullying can happen at any time and has the ability to reach a wide audience very quickly, often making its impact more intense and difficult to escape. These online interactions are often anonymous and this can embolden people to say things they might not say in person and for those being targeted, it can lead to feelings of isolation, anxiety and even depression.

As parents, what can you do?

It is important you remind your Teen that when online it can be easy to forget that some people don't have good intentions. From emails that may look real but are designed to steal your data, to people pretending to be someone else, knowing these threats exist is the first step in you helping your Teen protect themselves,

This isn't about creating fear of the online world, it is creating awareness for your Teen that the internet is the ideal place for people to pretend they are not who they appear to be and to falsely lead young and impressionable people to behave in a way that could be harmful to them, or others. The more you discuss the realities of what could happen, the more aware and prepared your Teen will be. Encourage them to talk to you about any concerns they have and if they are not sure about the intention of a conversation or a message they receive, to talk to you about it.

The need to protect personal and financial information has never been greater. Protecting personal and financial information is the first line of preventing that information falling into the wrong hands and being used for the fraudsters' own financial advantage.

These next three steps should be put in place as a matter of course to provide that layer of protection that has become so important in the fight back against online financial scams.

1.   **Passwords** - Talk to your Teen about the importance of having strong, unique passwords for each of their accounts and using multi-factor authentication when available. We all know the inconvenience of having to create and remember multiple passwords, but that inconvenience is nothing compared to what might have to be done if you or your Teen become the victim of a scam. There are a number of ways to ensure passwords are unique and can be stored safely and regularly updated. An app called LastPass is just one example.

2.   **Always keep financial information private** – Your Teen should never share bank or card details online, unless it's a secure trusted site. One way to know that a website is secure, is to ensure it starts with 'https'

at the beginning of the web address. If the 's' is missing, it means the site is not secure and your Teen should be told not to put any personal details onto that website.

It is also important that any documentation containing personal information including dates of birth, national insurance/identity numbers, passport details, bank account numbers or any numbers on a debit/ credit card, should always be securely destroyed and not simply screwed up and put into a bin. 'Bin diving' has become a well-known method for scammers to obtain personal details illegally and therefore you should advise your Teen to always ensure personal details cannot fall into the wrong hands.

3.   **Recognising suspicious activity** - Discuss with your Teen the warning signs on how to recognise phishing attempts, like unsolicited messages asking for sensitive information or links that don't match legitimate URLs.

Social Media – friend or foe?

There is no doubt that social media plays a huge role in teens' lives whether we like it or not. It offers countless opportunities for connection, self-expression and learning. However, it also presents potential risks, especially when it comes to online safety and scams. When parents talk to their Teens about these risks, framing social media as both a friend and a foe, can help teens approach it both with excitement and caution.

Of course, social media has incredible benefits. It allows teens to connect with friends, join supportive communities, explore interests and stay better informed. It can be a powerful tool for learning and sharing information; from school projects to hobbies and causes your Teen cares about. For many teens, it's also a place to build an online identity, which can be positive if approached with care.

When considering the role of social media as a friend, parents should emphasise the importance of using it to build meaningful connections and gain knew perspectives, while being absolutely mindful about what information they share. Encourage your Teen to think about privacy settings, selecting friends well and understanding that not everything online is as it seems. This can help your Teen create a safer and more positive online presence.

However, on the flip side as already discussed in this chapter, social media can also be an open gateway to potential scams, fake accounts and online predators who take advantage of young people's trust and openness. Scammers often disguise themselves as friendly peers, influencers, or even job recruiters and may draw teens into sharing personal information or clicking on harmful links. Ensuring your Teen has the awareness that, 'if it looks too good to be true it is' and urge them to question suspicious messages or offers, can help them to navigate social media with full awareness and a critical eye.

As a parent you can help your Teen understand that online friendships can be difficult, as not everyone is who they might claim to be. By asking questions like, 'would you trust this person if you met them in real life?', or 'does this seem like something a real friend would say or do?' You as a parent can encourage your Teen to assess their online relationships more critically.

As mentioned earlier in this chapter, remind your Teen of two questions that can be useful to ask in many situations, in this case to prevent them from becoming a victim of a scammer. They should simply ask themselves, 'is this possible?' and 'is it probable?'.

I certainly don't want teens becoming afraid of using social media, but as their parents it is your responsibility to ensure they do so as safely as possible.

How can you take a balanced approach?

1. **Set boundaries together** - encourage your Teen to set up privacy settings that limit who can contact them or see their posts. This can help prevent unwanted messages from strangers or suspicious accounts.
2. **Teach your Teen how to recognise red flags** - talk about the signs of scams, like being asked for personal information, money, or being encouraged to

click on unknown links. Share examples with your Teen that they might come across, to make these dangers more relatable for them.

3. **Encourage open communication** - let your Teen know they can always come to you if they feel uncomfortable or receive a suspicious message. The more they feel they can talk openly, without fear of judgement, the more likely they are to reach out to you, should something seem off.

4. **Promote digital literacy** - just as this book promotes financial literacy, it's also important that teens become savvy when it comes to online technology too. They should be encouraged to question what they see and who they interact with, especially online. Understanding how to 'fact check' and spot fake profiles or accounts empowers your Teen to make safer choices online.

5. **Managing friend requests and followers** – ask your Teen to only connect with people they know and trust, and to be cautious about strangers who reach out.

6. **What to do if your Teen encounters a scam** – encourage them to report suspicious accounts or

messages, ignore links and to speak to you if they are unsure.

7. **When in doubt, double check** – teach your Teen to verify unusual messages with the sender if they're claiming to be a friend, family member or reputable business.

8. **Responding to cyber bullying** – encourage your Teen to not engage with bullies and instead to block and report them or confide in you.

9. **Agree time boundaries together** - talk to your Teen about the importance of setting time limits for online activities, to reduce stress and maintain a healthy balance.

A great book I highly recommend is DOSE by TJ Power, which will help your Teen (and you if needed) to better manage their time online.

How to build strong habits for long term safety

The sooner you talk to your Teen about how to create a safe environment for themselves online, the sooner they can create healthy habits to protect themselves and to ensure they don't become a victim of a scam. There are a number of easy ways your Teen can do this:

- **Regularly review and update passwords and software** - explain to your Teen the importance of keeping devices secure by regularly updating passwords and software to prevent vulnerabilities.
- **Become a sceptic and always ask questions** - Encourage your Teen to always be curious, teach them to approach online interactions with a healthy dose of scepticism and encourage them to ask questions if they're unsure. The philosophy of 'no question is a silly question' is definitely one you should encourage them to adopt.
- **Stay informed about new scams and threats** - Online threats are evolving fast and staying informed is key to staying safe.

Online safety isn't a one-time thing, it's a habit. By advising your Teen to update passwords regularly, keep software current and remain cautious, you are helping them take control of their safety every day.

What to do if something goes wrong

As a parent it is also important to recognise that mistakes happen and no one is perfect. Encourage your Teen that if they feel something might be wrong, like an account being accessed or strange charges appearing, not to panic. They need to take fast action, by updating their passwords, contacting support and speaking to you or another trusted adult about the situation.

In the event of you or your Teen becoming a victim of a scam or recognising a scam is taking place, contact Action Fraud at the following address: https://www.actionfraud.police.uk/ if in the UK, or https://www.ftc.gov/ if in the USA.

CHAPTER 11

GROWING WEALTH TOGETHER AS A FAMILY

Earlier in the book I spoke about the importance of understanding your money mindset and I am going to return to this topic in this chapter. Wealth is an interesting word, as it can conjure up mixed emotions for many people, both positive and negative.

I want to start by defining what wealth is. Wealth is often thought of as having a lot of money, but it's actually a much broader concept. True wealth encompasses financial resources of course, but it also includes a sense of security, freedom and opportunity in life. It's the ability to not only afford what we need, but also to enjoy experiences, pursue goals and create a fulfilling lifestyle.

Wealth is often a misunderstood term and for those who have a relationship with money based on lack, the term wealth can lead them to associate negative feelings and behaviours with this word. Breaking down 'Maslow's Hierarchy of Needs' through the lens of wealth can help to illustrate how financial resources and security play a role in fulfilling each level of human need. This perspective can allow you to consider how wealth contributes not only to financial freedom but also to a more fulfilled and meaningful life. It is through this lens that I want you to consider the meaning of wealth.

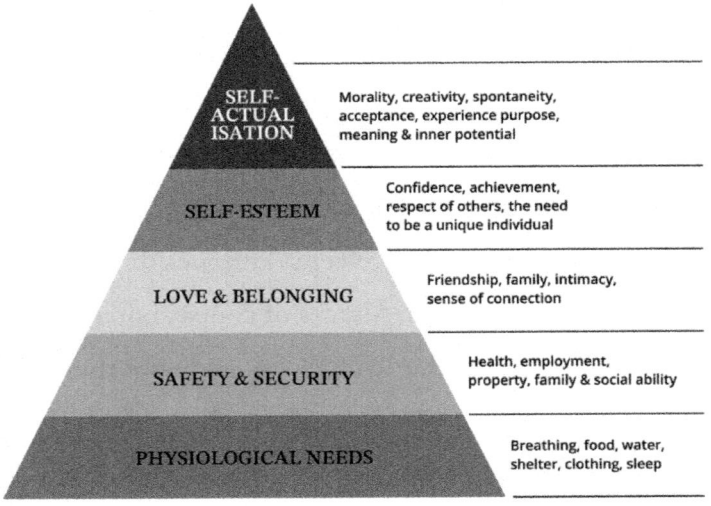

At the base of Maslow's pyramid are our physiological needs, the essentials that we need to survive like food, water, shelter and clothing. Wealth in its most basic form, allows us to secure these necessities. Financial resources provide the foundation to meet these primary needs without constant worry or uncertainty. When wealth meets these fundamental needs, it also allows individuals and families to focus on higher aspirations rather than just daily survival.

Wealth at this level
Income stability, budgeting for basic expenses and creating a financial foundation to support daily life.

Once our physical needs are met, the focus shifts to safety and security. In terms of wealth, this includes having a stable income, a home and savings for emergencies. Financial security provides a sense of safety that reduces stress and anxiety, allowing individuals to feel protected against life's uncertainties. This level of wealth enables individuals to plan for the future with confidence.

Wealth at this level
Emergency savings/soft landing fund, job security and plans for financial protection in uncertain times.

Next in Maslow's hierarchy of needs comes the need for connection and belonging. At the social level people seek relationships, community and a sense of belonging. Wealth can support these needs by enabling social experiences, like gathering with friends and family, participating in community events, or joining clubs and groups that create connections. Financial resources can also allow people to give back to their communities, support causes they care about and strengthen social ties.

Wealth at this level
Financial flexibility to engage in social activities, contribute to causes and build a network of supportive relationships.

Next let's look at our needs around achievement and self-worth. The need for esteem revolves around personal accomplishment, self-respect and recognition. At this level, wealth enables individuals to set and achieve financial goals, experience success and build self-confidence. For some this may mean investing in personal development, such as further education, certifications, or personal projects that bring a sense of achievement. Financial success at this level reinforces self-worth and motivates individuals to strive for higher goals.

Wealth at this level
Setting and achieving financial milestones, investing in self-improvement and building self-confidence, through personal and financial success.

At the top of Maslow's hierarchy is self-actualisation, which is the desire to reach your full potential and live a life of purpose and meaning. When wealth reaches this level, it allows individuals to focus on personal growth, creativity and fulfilling their passions. At this level, financial resources become a tool for realising dreams, contributing to society and making an impact that aligns with your values and life goals.

For many, self-actualisation, in terms of wealth, includes creating a legacy, building generational wealth, supporting causes, or pursuing creative projects that bring joy and fulfilment. This level is where wealth becomes not only about personal gain but also about using resources to make a difference in the world.

Wealth at this level
Investing in personal dreams, philanthropic efforts, supporting causes and building legacy for future generations.

By understanding wealth through Maslow's Hierarchy of Needs, I hope you can see that financial resource serves more than material purpose. Wealth supports every level of human need, helping us lead lives that are more secure, connected, purposeful and fulfilled. This perspective encourages a comprehensive approach to wealth, seeing it as a tool to enrich every aspect of life rather than simply an end goal.

By breaking down Maslow's Hierarchy of Needs simply in its explanation of wealth, please consider these points for the rest of this chapter:

- Financial wealth - beyond just money

- Emotional wealth - security and peace of mind
- Wealth - in time and freedom
- Wealth - in relationships and community
- Generational wealth - building for the future
- Personal fulfilment - wealth of purpose and joy

In this context when talking to teens about wealth, it's about creating a fulfilling, secure and meaningful life and financial literacy is a vital tool in making that happen. This perspective on wealth can help you and your family set richer, more meaningful financial goals together.

When families come together to grow wealth, they create a supportive environment where each person contributes, learns and gains from others in the process. Parents have the chance to model healthy financial habits, while teens can develop skills, confidence and a sense of responsibility. By approaching wealth building collectively, families can instil strong financial habits that will benefit not only today's generation but also the ones to come. The ripple effect is not only immediate but far-reaching and long-lasting. This journey becomes a legacy of knowledge, values and habits that can be passed down, creating lasting financial resilience.

This sense of creating a ripple effect is exactly what led me to write this book in the first place. As previously discussed in an earlier chapter, the majority of us were not taught about money at school. This may have led to feeling it was difficult to talk to your children about money, which just continues the cycle that had existed long before we were born.

The true power of collective financial growth lies in its ability to bring families closer together. Every financial decision, whether it's setting up a savings goal, discussing investments or planning for a family expense, becomes an opportunity to talk openly, work as a team and make decisions that reflect what's truly important. This kind of shared financial planning can further develop trust, accountability and a sense of unity. Families who build wealth together, tend to create a strong foundation of financial habits and values, which not only helps them achieve financial security, but also gives them the freedom to pursue experiences, dreams and goals that enhance their lives.

I want to explore now how families can take on wealth building as a collaborative effort, harnessing the strengths, perspectives and dreams of each family member. By understanding the power of collective financial growth, families can create a positive, supportive environment that encourages learning, responsible decision making and a vision for financial freedom that benefits everyone. As you read on, you'll discover practical ways to set financial goals, build sustainable habits and create a wealth mindset that lasts for generations.

Setting Shared Financial Goals

Building wealth as a family begins with setting shared financial goals that everyone can work towards together. When teens are actively involved in setting these goals, they not only gain valuable financial skills, but also a sense of ownership and responsibility. Setting shared goals helps everyone feel like a valued part of the family's financial journey, building a foundation of trust and shared commitment.

Involving your Teen in setting financial goals, which

lead to family wealth, is a fantastic practical way to involve them in a skill that will serve them for life and beyond as they will go on to teach their family this same approach.

Involving teens in family financial planning helps them understand the importance of saving, budgeting and making thoughtful decisions. As a parent, start by having an open conversation about your family's financial priorities, inviting your Teen to share their thoughts and ideas. Discussing goals with your Teen helps them to feel more invested in the results and they'll learn first-hand about the steps needed to reach those goals.

Encourage teens to contribute their own ideas, whether it's saving for a family trip, putting aside money for a charitable cause, or starting to save for higher education. This involvement makes financial goals feel more achievable and will help your Teen to understand that money isn't just a tool for individual gain, but also a way to accomplish meaningful experiences and support each other. As we know teens can be selfish, so this collective approach to setting family goals is a great way to encourage them to look beyond just their own needs.

Examples of possible family goals

Creating goals that are SMART, in other words Specific, Measurable, Achievable, Realistic, Time-bound and ensuring they are aligned with family values, can make the process both rewarding and motivating for everyone. Here are some examples of achievable goals you might set together:

1. **Saving for a family holiday** - decide as a family where you would like to go, then break down the savings target into monthly or weekly contributions. This goal teaches everyone about planning for future experiences and working together toward something enjoyable.

2. **Contributing to a charity or good cause** - together as a family choose a charity or cause that matters to you all and set a target amount to donate. Teens can help research organisations, plan fund raising activities, or even suggest ways to save up in order to contribute. This will allow teens to look beyond their own needs and to be aware of their own fortune in

comparison to others, who may be less fortunate than them.

3. **Investing in long-term assets** - discuss the idea of investing for the future, such as starting an education fund, a family emergency fund or even a small investment account for the teen. Set a realistic target and agree on monthly contributions. This goal introduces teens to the concept of investing and the power of building wealth over time. You can take this a step further as a family, by researching the best options for your money and involving a trusted advisor at this stage also.

Exercise - Setting Three Shared Financial Goals

Revisit the exercise set in Chapter 5 and this time look at making goal setting a meaningful family activity. Take time to brainstorm and decide on three shared financial goals. They may be the same three goals as you previously discussed or they may now, with the additional information and conversations that you have had during the reading of this book, be different goals. As you go through this exercise consider each goal's purpose, timeframe and the specific steps everyone can take to contribute.

Step 1. Identify the goals

- Goal 1 - A short-term goal e.g., saving for a family outing or holiday celebration.
- Goal 2 - A medium-term goal e.g., contributing to a charity or setting up a home improvement fund.
- Goal 3 - A long-term goal e.g., building an education fund or investing in a family savings account.

Step 2. Discuss the purpose of each goal

- Together talk about why each goal is important. Ask questions like, "What do we hope to gain from achieving this goal?" and, "How does this goal align with our family/our own values?" This step helps reinforce that financial goals aren't just about money but about creating opportunities and building a future together.

Step 3. Set timelines for each goal

- Decide on realistic timelines for each goal. For example, a short-term goal might be achievable in three to six months, while a long-term goal could take several years to achieve. By setting timelines, you create clear expectations and can create milestones you can celebrate together as a family along the way.

Step 4. Outline everyone's role and contribution

- Define how each family member will contribute, whether it's directly through saving, budgeting, or coming up with creative ideas to reach the target. For example, teens might commit to setting aside a portion of their allowance or help plan budget friendly activities to increase savings. This has the additional benefit of encouraging teens to become more mindful with regards to saving money, also how they spend money and may even influence how their parents spend money. It can also highlight the benefits of delayed gratification, e.g., deciding not to purchase something now, but instead put that money towards other goals, that the family have agreed on.

Step 5. Monitor progress together

- Track your progress as a family, checking in regularly to see how close you are to reaching each goal. It's really important to celebrate small wins, make adjustments as needed and keep the conversation open. This tracking process teaches accountability and reinforces that building wealth is a step-by-step journey.

Setting financial goals as a family creates connection, discipline and a shared sense of achievement. By working together towards these targets, teens learn valuable money management skills, which will benefit them throughout their life, while the family strengthens its financial foundations and bonds.

Learning about investment basics as a family

For many parents, the idea of talking to their Teens about investing might feel intimidating. If you're a parent who hasn't discussed money or investing with your Teen before, you're not alone. It's common to feel like you need to be an expert to teach these topics, but the truth is, you don't. The most important thing is your willingness to learn together. Exploring investment basics as a family can be a fun and enlightening experience, building confidence for both you and your Teen as you discover what investing is all about.

Investment fundamentals explained for teens (and parents!)

When we talk about investing, we're referring to the process of using money to earn more over time. Unlike simply saving, which involves setting money aside for a future purpose, investing is about growing that money, by putting it to work in different assets. Let's explore a few common types of investments with some simple analogies to make them easier to understand.

1. Shares - Owning a tiny piece of a company

Analogy - imagine you're part of a garden club where everyone has a small plot. Each member's plot represents a share of the whole garden and if the garden produces fruit or flowers, everyone enjoys part of the harvest.

Explanation - Shares represent small ownership shares in a company. When you buy a share (or stock as it's called in the USA), you own a tiny piece of that business. If the company does well, the share value can increase, allowing you to earn money if you decide to sell it later.

2. Bonds - Lending money and earning interest

Analogy - think of bonds like lending a friend some money to help them bake a cake. In return, they promised to pay you back with a small extra slice of cake, as a thank you for your help.

Explanation - Bonds are like loans you give to a company or government. When you buy a bond, you're essentially lending money to an organisation and in return, they pay you back with interest over time. Bonds tend to be lower risk than shares, making them a safer but slower growing investment.

3. Mutual Funds - Teaming up to grow money

Analogy – Imagine you and a group of friends each contribute ingredients to bake a batch of cookies. When the cookies are ready, you all share in the final result. This way, everyone benefits without needing all the ingredients or skills.

Explanation - Mutual Funds are collections of investments like shares and bonds that are pooled together. Investors buy into the fund, which is managed by professionals who choose a variety of assets. By investing in a mutual fund, you get the advantage of having a piece of many different investments, spreading out risk.

Family activity
Pick and follow a share, company, or asset together as a

family.

Learning about investing becomes much more engaging when you see how investments change over time. This activity encourages your family to pick a share, a well-known company, or an asset to follow together, learning about its performance, what affects its value and how investing can be a long-term process.

How to get started

1.   Pick a Share or company

Choose a familiar company that everyone recognises and is interested in. Think of brands you use every day, like a favourite tech company, a popular clothing brand, or a company known for its snacks or games. This familiarity will make it easier for everyone to relate to the activity and stay engaged.

2.   Set up a weekly check-in

Each week, check the company's share price or value and record it. Look up any recent news about the company, such as new product launches or financial reports and discuss how these events might affect the share's value. Remember that share prices go up and down all the time, which is normal in the world of investing.

Discuss the ups and downs. Together talk about what you observe. When the share price goes up, discuss why it might have increased. When it goes down, explore the reasons and remind everyone that investing is a long game where ups and downs are part of the journey.

3. **Explore key investment lessons together**
   - *Patience* - Investing is usually about growth over time, so don't expect quick returns.
   - *Research* - the more you learn about a company or interesting industry, the better your understanding of its long-term potential.
   - *Risk and Reward* - Some investments are riskier than others, but with more risk can come higher potential returns.

4. **Reflect on the experience as a family**
At the end of a few months, review what you have learnt. How did following a stock or company help your

family understand investing? Discuss whether anyone would consider investing in that share or fund for real, or if there are other companies or assets that seem more attractive.

This activity will give your family a hands-on way to explore investing without any pressure to be experts. By learning together, you and your Teen can become more confident in their financial knowledge, understanding that wealth building is a skill that anyone can learn, one step at a time.

But one word of caution, remember to only invest what you can afford and that what you invest in can go down as well as up. This is why practising the activity I have just shared with you will give you the opportunity to 'play and learn' in a completely safe way, before deciding what you want to do next. Also note, it is possible to invest from as little as £1, so beginning your investment journey can start in a small practical and safe way.

Building a family budget

Budgeting is one of the most important tools for managing money and building a family budget brings everyone into the financial planning process. When budgeting is done together, it becomes more than just managing money. It's an opportunity for each family member to learn, contribute and understand how their financial choices affect everyone. By creating a family budget, parents can model good financial habits and teens can see first-hand how intentional planning supports everyone's goals and well-being.

Budgeting as a family allows everyone to see the bigger picture of household expenses and goals. It's a reminder that each expense can affect the family as a whole, helping teens appreciate the cost of everyday items and understand the balance between wants and needs. Collaborative budgeting also opens the door for honest conversations about money, giving teens a sense of responsibility and ownership over the family's financial health.

When teens participate in budgeting, they learn how to

set limits, prioritise spending and make choices that reflect the families shared values and goals. This experience provides them with money management skills they can apply throughout their lives, helping them to become financially responsible adults.

How to design a collaborative budget

Creating a family budget can be fun, educational and rewarding. Here are some tips to make it a positive experience for everyone:

1. Assign roles and responsibilities

- To make the budget truly collaborative, assign each family member a role or specific category to manage. For example, one person could be responsible for tracking entertainment costs, whilst another keeps an eye on groceries. Teens can take ownership of categories they're interested in, like outings with friends or family activities, to help them see the impact of everyday spending.

2.   **Set realistic budget categories**

- Use categories that make sense for your family's spending patterns. Common categories include:

- Groceries - Essential for daily living and teens can help plan meals within the grocery budget.
- Entertainment - Activities like films, sport, or family outings. Teens can contribute by finding affordable or free options.
- Savings - setting aside a portion of income for future needs, emergencies, or shared family goals.
- Donations - If your family values giving back, set a budget for charitable contributions and let your Teens help choose causes to support.

3.   **Hold regular check-ins**

- Schedule monthly or weekly check-ins to review how the family is sticking to the budget. These meetings are a chance to celebrate any savings, discuss adjustments and make decisions. Check-ins help reinforce that budgeting is an ongoing process that requires attention, adjustments and a positive attitude. It's not about restriction, but education.

4. Celebrate small wins together

- Budgeting as a family can be challenging, but every small win deserves recognition. When the family stays under budget for a category or achieves a saving goal, take a moment to celebrate. This reinforces good habits and shows that budgeting leads to rewards, beyond just saving money.

"Let's Talk!"

Exercise - Create a monthly family budget

This exercise will guide your family through creating a monthly budget, discussing needs, wants and future goals along the way. It's a hands-on activity that teaches everyone about planning and prioritising expenses.

Step 1. Create a list of money income and expenses

- Start by listing all sources of family income for the month. This can include salaries, freelance work, benefits, allowances and any additional earnings.

- Next, make a list of regular monthly expenses. Include fixed costs like rent or mortgage payments, utilities and other recurring bills. Then add variable expenses like groceries, entertainment and savings.

Step 2. Divide expenses into needs, wants and goals

- Work together to categorise each expense:

    o **Needs** - Essentials for living, such as housing, groceries and utilities.

    o **Wants** – Non-essential but enjoyable expenses, like eating out, going to the cinema or subscriptions.

    o **Goals Future** - focused items, like savings, education funds, or a family holiday fund.

- Discuss each category and talk about why it's important to prioritise needs first, set aside funds for goals and manage wants with balance.

Step 3. Assign categories and responsibilities

- Give each family member a budget category to manage. Teens can be responsible for entertainment, groceries or even a small portion of savings. Encourage them to look for ways to save or make budget-friendly choices within their category, which can help them develop practical money management skills.

Step 4. Set spending limits and saving targets

- Together, set realistic spending limits for each category based on your total income and expenses. For example, decide on a fixed amount for entertainment and a grocery budget and a target for savings. This teaches everyone to work within a limit and understand the importance of planning and compromise.

Step 5. Review and adjust each month

- Each month, come together to review how well the family stuck to the budget. Discuss any areas where you overspent or underspent and adjust the next month's budget accordingly. This process emphasises that budgeting is flexible and adaptable, depending on the family's changing needs and goals.

Building a family budget together creates transparency, accountability and mutual support. Teens gain invaluable budgeting experience and families learn how to plan and save with purpose. By approaching budgeting as a shared responsibility, families not only improve their financial well-being but also build a culture of open communication, teamwork and lasting financial habits.

Encourage an entrepreneurial spirit

Reading the book *Rich Dad, Poor Dad* by Robert Kiyosaki in 2020, totally changed the way my husband and I parent our children. I was brought up with the belief that I had to work hard at school, go to university and then take my place on the corporate ladder. I believed this was the only route to success. In fairness this route did serve me well (to an extent) and I believed it was important that I raised my two boys to follow the same path as me.

However, whilst reading *Rich Dad, Poor Dad*, I became very aware that there was more than one singular route to success. In the book, Kiyosaki contrasts two different approaches to money management and wealth building, as learnt from his own father and father figure experience.

In the book, 'Poor Dad' represents Kiyosaki's biological father, a highly educated public servant who believed in working hard, saving money and playing it safe with finances. Despite his intelligence, he struggled financially and taught Kiyosaki the conventional wisdom of 'go to school, get a good job and retire securely'.

'Rich Dad' is Kiyosaki's friend's father, a self-made millionaire with limited formal education. He

encouraged entrepreneurial thinking, investing and
building passive income streams. Rich Dad's lessons
focused on financial literacy, understanding assets and
liabilities and making money work for you.

Such was the power of the examples shared in this
book, I actively and quickly changed my approach to
how I encouraged my children. Yes, I still wanted them
to work hard and do well at school, as I believe this
would present them with more options on what they
decided to do with their lives. However, I no longer
believe it is imperative for them to go on to university
and then secure a job within a corporate business.
Instead, I have encouraged them to consider the
possibility of a more entrepreneurial life. After all, this
will be the only life my sons will remember their parents
living.

I was surprised by how quickly I recognised the
limitations I had placed on myself by working for
someone else. The structure and constraints of
employment had shaped the way I lived my life, and it
wasn't until I started running my own business that I
truly experienced the freedom of making decisions for

myself, my family, and my future.

I still want my sons to understand the value of working in a corporate environment, as it can be an excellent training ground. I also want them to see that there are other paths available to them. My hope is that they recognise these possibilities sooner than I did.

I would highly recommend that you read *Rich Dad, Poor Dad*, but I also encourage you to share your copy of the book with your Teen. But until you have the opportunity to read it for yourself, I would like to share the five key lessons I took from the book:

- **Financial education is a non-negotiable** - As not enough schools teach effective money management, it is vital your Teen starts and continues their own education on this topic. My book is a great start, but the journey begins rather than ends here.
- **Assets vs Liabilities** - Assets put money in your pocket e.g., investments, savings etc., whilst liabilities take money away e.g., loans and unnecessary expenses.

- **The 'Rat Race'** - This concept features heavily in Kiyosaki's book and hit me hard. Many people get stuck in a cycle of earning and spending without building wealth. They do it automatically and subconsciously a lot of the time, without even realising it.
- **The power of entrepreneurship and investing** - Kiyosaki believes it vital to build passive income, which is key to financial freedom.
- **Mindset shift** – Kiyosaki, like me, is a big believer in 'what you think you become' and wealth begins with a change in thinking, from working for money to making money work for you.

To summarise, the book emphasises that taking calculated risks, learning continuously and adopting a proactive approach, is key to achieving financial independence. For me, it was an inspiring and timely call to action for anyone looking to rethink their relationship with money.

CHAPTER 12
CONVERSATIONS WITH YOUR FUTURE SELF

As an author, I am not sure I should be admitting to a favourite chapter, they are all good, but connecting with the power of your Future Self is something I believe can be game-changing for you as a parent, but for your Teen as well.

But be prepared; as the parent, it will be a concept that you will find easier to work with, than your Teen, who is just starting to come to terms with this new stage in their life. Asking them to think beyond even tomorrow may take some encouragement and positive reinforcement. But stick with it, as your Teen's Future Self will thank you, eventually.

Visualising your Future Self is powerful, because it creates the bridge between your present behaviour and long-term goals. If you are able to make a connection between what you are doing now and what can benefit you in the future, this can make it easier to take what might otherwise be a hard step.

Being able to visualise your future and encouraging your Teen to do the same, has several significant benefits.

1.   Creates clarity and direction

Visualising your Future Self is a powerful way to understand and find out what you truly want to achieve. This clarity can help provide a road map on the action you need to take instead of allowing vague aspirations. You have a specific actionable set of goals which can be the catalyst for making sure they happen.

2.   Supports long term thinking

Visualising shifts your focus from the here and now and immediate gratification, towards long-term, sustainable success. By imagining the rewards and the joy your

Future Self can look forward to, you're more likely to prioritise decisions that align with your long-term goals.

3.   Increases self-control

Research shows that people who feel connected to their future selves make better choices about their money and life in general. Visualising your Future Self creates a stronger emotional connection, making it easier to delay impulsive decisions or unnecessary spending in favour of future benefits.

4.   Creates motivation and accountability

Taking the time to imagine the life you want creates a real sense of excitement and purpose. You're more likely to take responsibility for your actions when you can see how they directly impact the person you want to become.

I visualise a physical connection between my Future Self and I, like an invisible thread. This thread provides a constant reminder, linking the here and now to what I want to be experiencing in the future. This creates accountability to my Future Self, to ensure I am taking the necessary action for her to be enjoying the future I am imagining for her.

5. Helps overcome fear and uncertainty

Visualising your Future Self leading a life where you are thriving, despite challenges, builds confidence in your ability to navigate setbacks. It also reinforces the belief that your efforts today are worthwhile and achievable. Creating a real connection between now and your future can help to enhance not only your future but the here and now.

6. Aligning daily action-taking with aspiration

Just like an athlete imagines themselves crossing the finish line first, visualising your Future Self achieving all the goals you are setting for yourself is a proven way to align the action you are taking on a daily basis, with the aspiration you have for your Future Self. I strongly recommend that you put aside some dedicated time every day to connect with your Future Self and the kind of life you want to be leading in your future. I would then recommend you have the same conversation with your Teen and encourage them to do the same. This will lead to beautiful conversations between you and your Teen allowing both of you to deeply explore the kind of life you both want to be living and how you are going to make it happen.

7. Create positive habits

When you imagine your Future Self enjoying the results of habits you are creating now like saving, budgeting or investing, it becomes easier to start those behaviours. The visualisation creates a tangible emotional reward, making it more likely you will stick to these habits, both now and in the future.

8. Supports emotional well-being

By visualising a successful future, you boost hope and optimism which in turn develops resilience, as you're reminded of your own growth and potential, which is waiting for you on the other side of challenges.

By regularly visualising your Future Self, you are

creating a mental blueprint that guides your actions in the here and now, but also ensures they are aligned with your values and aspirations for the future. It's a powerful tool for building Money Confidence and achieving the life you imagine.

How to have a conversation with your Future Self and encourage your Teen to do the same

Talking to your Future Self is a powerful way to imagine the life you want to create and align the actions you take with your goals and dreams. However, as a parent, this exercise isn't just for you, it's a fantastic tool to share with your Teen. It helps them to develop a sense of direction and ownership over their future.

I am sure you can recall how it felt to be a teen. The future was something that happened to old people and we never gave it very much thought. However, with experience, we know time does fly by and therefore, the sooner we can take responsibility for the kind of life we want to be living in the future, the sooner we can make that our reality.

This is why talking to your Teen about their Future Self

and helping them to connect with that future sooner rather than later will help them more quickly take full advantage of what visualising and connecting with that future can bring.

So, let's explore exactly how you can have those conversations with your Future Self and then help your Teen to do the same.

Step 1. Start with you

Before encouraging your Teen to have this conversation, it's important that you experience it for yourself. When you model this exercise, you're not only putting yourself in the position of being better equipped to guide them, but you are also able to demonstrate the value of reflecting on your future.

How to begin your conversation

1. Find a quiet space and take a few deep breaths to centre yourself.

2. Picture yourself five, ten, or even twenty years into the future. Visualise your life at that point in time. How are you spending your time? What is happening with regards to your relationships, health and happiness?

3. Imagine your Future Self as someone who has achieved all the goals you care about most.

4. Ask yourself:

    - What advice does my Future Self have for me today?
    - What does my Future Self want me to focus on to make the most progress?
    - What does my Future Self want me to stop worrying about?

Write down whatever comes to mind, with no judgement, as these reflections can offer clarity and motivation.

Step 2. Introduce this Idea to your Teen

Approach this exercise with curiosity and enthusiasm. Teens often appreciate activities that feel meaningful but are also fun and creative.

Conversation Starters

- "Have you ever thought about what your life might be like in 10 years?"
- "I did this interesting exercise where I imagined talking to myself in the future. It helped me to work out what's important to me. Would you like to give it a try together?"

Step 3. Guide Your Teen through the visualisation

Help your Teen imagine their Future Self. Make it a relaxed, low-pressure activity. Encourage them to close their eyes, take a few deep breaths and picture their life ten years from now.

Prompt questions for your Teen:

- **What does your Future Self look like? Where are you?**
- **What are you doing with your time?**
- **Who are the people around you?**
- **What are you doing that you enjoy?**
- **What makes you feel proud or happy in your future life?**

Remember there are no right or wrong answers and reassure your Teen of the same. This is about their dreams and feelings.

Step 4. Facilitate the conversation

Encourage your Teen to imagine sitting down with their Future Self for a friendly chat. Ask them to think about what their Future Self might say to guide them today.

I use a very similar approach with my clients, utilising something called the 'Rocking Chair Coach'. This is where you imagine yourself walking into a dimly lit room and at the far end of the room you see an older person sitting in a rocking chair. You vaguely recognise the person in the chair, and you move closer towards them. As you start to come into their line of vision, they smile at you warmly as they recognise who you are. At the same time, you realise who they are. The person in the rocking chair is you aged 80 years old, and they want to provide you with all the answers to the questions that you have for your Future Self.

I don't recommend asking your Teen to look this far into the future at this stage, depending on their age. I would suggest initially looking no further out than 10 years into the future. This is far enough out to give your Teen some perspective but not so far out into the future that they feel it too hard to imagine ever happening.

Here are some suggested questions for teens to ask their Future Self:

- What advice would you give me about what I'm doing now?

- What habits helped you get to where you are today?
- Is there anything you wish I would start or stop doing?
- What's something I'm worrying about now, that won't matter in the future?

Step 5. Share your own experiences

After your Teen has had their reflection, share some of what you learnt when you did the same exercise. This can help normalise the process and make it feel less pressured and intimidating.

For example:

'When I asked my Future Self what I should focus on, they reminded me to stop stressing about small setbacks and focus on the bigger picture. It really helped me to rethink my goals.'

Step 6. Help Your Teen reflect and act

Encourage your Teen to write down what their Future Self shared with them. Then discuss what actions they can take today to move closer to the future they imagined for themselves.

Reflection prompts for teens:

- What stood out the most from your conversation with your Future Self?
- What's one thing you can start doing today to work towards your goals?
- How does imagining your Future Self make you feel about your current choices?

Step 7. Make it an ongoing practice

Let your Teen know they can revisit this exercise anytime they want to. As they grow and their goals evolve, so will their conversations with their Future Self. You can even set a date to do it together again, perhaps annually or even at the start of a new school year.

Why this matters

For both you and your Teen, having a conversation with your Future Self creates a real sense of direction, accountability as well as self-awareness. It's a way to connect with your goals, break them into actionable steps and build confidence in your ability to shape your future.

By doing this exercise together, you're not only helping your Teen develop a vision for their future but also strengthening your bond, as you grow and learn alongside each other.

Your Future Self and your Teen's Future Self are cheering you on. Every decision you make has the power to move you closer to the life you imagine. So, sit down, have that conversation and take the first step towards becoming the person you're destined to be.

The bridge between now and the future

You must identify the current actions, habits and choices that will shape your financial journey and that of your Teen as well. This will act as the bridge between the here and now and the future. These daily decisions, whether conscious or unconscious create the foundation for your future financial reality. Think of them as the planks of a bridge, connecting where you stand today to where you aspire to be tomorrow. By intentionally building this bridge with purpose and clarity, you not only strengthen your own financial path, but also empower your Teen to walk confidently toward their own financial independence.

To help with the process of creating a bridge, the Future Self map is a really helpful exercise to complete with your Teen:

- Define three to five key goals for the future e.g., buying a home, building an emergency/soft landing fund, travelling, supporting family etc.
- Outline the specific actions needed today to achieve those goals.
- Include checkpoints to reassess and celebrate progress.

You can both complete this exercise independently and then come together to discuss what you have each written, or you can take it in turn to answer each question together. Whichever way you choose to complete this exercise, I recommend you write down each of your answers so you can come back to them at a later point.

Building Money Confidence with your Future Self in mind

Developing Money Confidence isn't just about understanding numbers or making financial decisions today, it's about creating a mindset and habits that align with the life you imagine for your Future Self. By anchoring your financial choices to a vision of where you want to be, you make each action more purposeful, transforming small daily decisions into powerful steps towards financial security and freedom. And when you model this approach for your Teen, you provide them with the tools to do the same.

Why Your Future Matters

Your Future Self is the person you're working toward becoming, the version of you who has achieved financial goals, overcome challenges and built a life that reflects your values and priorities. When you make decisions with this person in mind, you create a sense of accountability and alignment between your present and future.

However, as a parent, you have more financial mistakes to learn from than your Teen does right now. This creates a fantastic opportunity for them to build their future with intention and confidence, designing a life on their terms in a way you may not have been able to until now.

When you and your Teen make decisions with each of your Future Selves in mind, you can both create a sense of accountability and alignment between your present and future.

For example:

- Saving for a rainy day isn't just about money, it's about giving your Future Self peace of mind and financial security.
- Choosing to invest in learning a new skill is an investment in the opportunities and growth your Future Self will enjoy.

Helping your Teen understand this concept can inspire them to think long term, even as they navigate the short-term temptations and pressures that come with quite simply, being a teen.

Transforming reflection into action

It isn't just enough to connect with your vision of the future, it's time to translate those insights into action and it's important that you encourage your Teen to do the same. Building Money Confidence requires consistency and intention and it's about focusing on progress, not perfection.

Ideas for daily Money Confidence builders

- **Track your spending**

Understand where your money goes and align your spending with your goals and values. Remember your Future Self; will your spending habits now support you to create the sort of life you previously envisaged for your Future Self?

- **Practise gratitude**

Focus on what you have already, instead of what you lack, reducing the urge to overspend.

- **Set small, achievable goals**

Start with realistic goals that build momentum, like saving an extra amount a week, or reducing a recurring expense.

Encourage your Teen to take similar action, such as saving a portion of their allowance or if they already have a part-time job their salary, or tracking their spending habits. Ideally, they would be doing both.

Help them set small financial goals that feel achievable and can help further develop their confidence.

Teens often struggle to connect their current decisions to their future outcomes. By introducing the idea of their Future Self, you can help them see how their actions today can shape their opportunities tomorrow.

Ways to support your Teen:

- **Model Money Confidence**

Share your own experiences - both successes and challenges. The more you can model your own experiences and be honest about the highs and the lows, the more confidence your Teen will have in terms of what your expectations are for them and how you are open to have these conversations with them.

- **Encourage them to continue to visualise**

I have already talked about the power of imagination and connecting with your Future Self, continue to do this frequently yourself and encourage your Teen to do the same. This will allow them to see how what they do today and the actions they take, will have a positive or otherwise outcome for their Future Self.

- **Teach them to plan**

The concept of Future Self is likely to be a new one for your Teen, therefore they are going to need support to break their goals down into manageable steps, such as saving for a specific item, or learning about investing. Continue to encourage them to be open, to ask questions and be curious. Always.

Celebrating the journey

Building Money Confidence with your Future Self in mind is not about achieving perfection, it's about creating a sense of progress and purpose. It is important to celebrate milestones along the way, whether it's paying off a debt, hitting a savings target, or simply feeling more in control of your finances.

For your Teen, recognise their efforts no matter how small. Acknowledge when they make a smart money decision or demonstrate an understanding of long-term thinking. Positive reinforcement helps build confidence and encourages them to keep learning and growing.

The ripple effect

When you build Money Confidence with your Future Self in mind, you are inspiring your Teen to do the same. By modelling a proactive, future focused mindset, you show them financial success is attainable and it starts with the choices they make today.

Together, you create a legacy of financial literacy, empowerment and independence, one decision, one habit and one step at a time.

Your Future Self should not be considered a distant stranger, he or she is the version of you that depends on the actions you take today. Build a relationship with them, keep their dreams in focus and let them inspire you to make confident, intentional money decisions. When you do, you will not only create a better future for yourself, but also for your Teen; empowering them to approach their financial journey with clarity and confidence.

Writing a letter to your Future Self

This is an exercise I particularly like and recommend to my clients to do every year on the 1st of January; draft a letter to their Future Self. This is a powerful way to connect with what your intentions are for the future year and to congratulate yourself on all that you are going to achieve.

Write the letter from the perspective of already having achieved the goals and aspirations that you have for yourself for the next 12 months. Include your hopes, dreams and financial goals. Celebrate yourself and show gratitude for everything you have done leading up to this point that has allowed you to achieve the success that you are going to have over the next 12 months (as though you have already achieved it).

Once you have drafted the letter, go to the website *www.futureme.org*, create an e-mail from the draft and send it to yourself. Set the timer on the website to return your e-mail to you 12 months later.

This acts as a brilliant accountability tool, as you know

what goals you are working towards over the next 12 months. Knowing you are going to receive an e-mail from your Future Self in 12 months' time, congratulating you on what you have achieved, should be enough motivation to help you stick to what you need to do.

Depending on the time that you are reading this book, will be the deciding factor on what date you choose to send your letter to your Future Self. I always choose the 1st of January to write my letter and to receive the one from the previous year. Although a very simple tool, it is highly effective and great for self-accountability.

Again, I highly recommend you encourage your Teen to complete this exercise as well, however, why not take it a stage further by sharing each other's letter, as this adds an extra level of accountability and support.

Paying it forward – Learning to share knowledge & confidence

For too long we have been let down by the education system when it comes to teaching children about money. This stops with you and your Teen. Gaining financial knowledge and creating Money Confidence is a transformative journey, but its true power lies in what you do with it. By taking what you've learnt and sharing it with others e.g., your family, friends and the next generation, be under no illusion you can create a ripple effect that extends far beyond your own life. In doing so, you help break the cycle of money being a taboo subject and you will no longer be reliant on somebody else teaching you (or indeed up until now, not teaching you) about money and how to effectively manage it.

Through the knowledge you have gained in this book and the exercises you and your Teen have completed, you will be able to contribute to making financial literacy accessible to everyone. This book aims to show every single parent they have the ability to not only become financially competent themselves, but to support their Teen to do the same and for both of you to become money confident.

So, let's look in more detail at how you can now pay it forward and become part of the solution in terms of creating true financial empowerment for a much wider community of people. It can start with you.

Breaking the taboo

For too many generations, money has often been seen as a subject to avoid; too personal, too difficult, or too uncomfortable to discuss. What has this silence done for us? Absolutely nothing. Silence only perpetuates fear, shame and misinformation around finances. But worse than that it prevents us from being fully in control of our lives. Money is not the be all and end all, however having money, being able to effectively manage and control money, gives us choices. By openly discussing money with those around you, you challenge this norm and pave the way for more informed, empowered conversations.

And why does this matter?

- Transparency creates trust - talking about money creates openness, allowing us to learn from each other and share valuable experience and insights.

- Shared knowledge benefits everyone - the financial world can be intimidating, but sharing your experiences can help others navigate it more confidently. Remember there are only a few key things you need to know to successfully manage your money. This approach helps create confidence to ask questions and be curious, because you do not need to be the expert, you just need to have the confidence to find the right expert and to ask the right questions.

- Empowerment through education - the more you talk about money, the more you normalise the conversation for everyone. This in turn encourages other people to ask questions and be curious and to educate themselves as a result.

Supporting friends and family

Your journey towards Money Confidence provides you with the tools to benefit those closest to you. Whether it's continuing to have the conversation with your Teen, helping a sibling understand budgeting, guiding a friend through saving for a big purchase, or discussing long-term financial planning with a partner, sharing your knowledge strengthens your relationships and empowers those around you.

Ways to support others

- **Be approachable -** Let friends and family know they can talk to you about money without judgement. When people know a subject is not off the table and can be discussed, this can lead to a more open conversation and the opportunity for people to become much more open with regards to how they talk about money with others.
- **Share your experiences** – People welcome learning from others through sharing of real-life examples about what has worked for them and what hasn't.
- **Encourage open conversations** - Start discussions about financial goals, challenges and successes during family gatherings or casual

chats. You don't need to plan a conversation specifically around money, as this can lead to uncomfortable discussions and fear of judgement. However, if the topic is 'brought up' casually, it can be seen as just having a normal discussion.

Empowering the next generation

One of the best ways to pay it forward is by empowering the next generation with financial literacy. Too many young people enter adulthood without a clear understanding of how to manage money, often learning through costly mistakes. Just like many parents did before them and their parents before them. By giving your Teen and other young people in your life the tools to make informed decisions, you are directly helping them on a path to financial independence and success.

I invite you to pause and reflect at this point on how far you and your Teen have come to reach this point and the effect you can now have on the next generation.

What can I do?

You may be feeling like a bit of an impostor right now, asking yourself, "How can I even think I have the knowledge and experience to empower the next generation?" However, I hope this book has taught you that you don't need to be an expert to manage your finances and to start to feel more confident about managing your money going forward.

This is not a journey with a final destination. By paying it forward, you contribute to breaking the cycle of financial illiteracy. This isn't just about passing down tips or tricks, it's about creating a culture where money is no longer taboo, where financial knowledge is shared freely and where everyone feels empowered to take control of their financial future. Actually, it's more than that, I see it as people taking back control of their financial future and not allowing anyone else to make those decisions for them.

Let's look at the impact of sharing your financial knowledge

- **The narrative that has been handed down generation to generation** - Your efforts can shift how your family and community approach money for years to come.
- **Build stronger communities** - Financially confident individuals contribute to more stable and resilient communities.
- **Inspiring a movement** - Every conversation you have about money helps normalise it as an essential skill. By you sharing your knowledge, asking questions, being curious and encouraging those around you, this helps others to do the same.

How to start paying it forward

If you are unsure where to begin, start small. Sharing your knowledge does not have to be scary or overwhelming. It's about creating meaningful connections and offering support where it's needed.

Here are some practical ways to start paying it forward:

- Host a family money talk to discuss shared goals or lessons learnt.
- Mentor a young person on how to save for their first big purchase or manage their first salary.
- Share your favourite financial book, podcast or tools with friends. There are many exercises in this book for you to share and recommend.

The ripple effect of giving back

When you pay it forward, the impact reaches far beyond the person you're helping. The knowledge and confidence you share will inspire them to do the same for others. This creates a ripple effect, gradually changing how money is discussed, understood and managed within families, communities and society as a whole. Building Money Confidence with your Future Self in mind is a transformative process. But the greatest gift is using that confidence to lift others, breaking down barriers and building bridges toward financial literacy for everyone. By sharing your knowledge, you're not just creating a better financial future for yourself and your Teen, you're inspiring a legacy of openness, empowerment and financial change that will resonate for generations to come.

As we reach the end of this book, remember that this isn't the conclusion - it's the beginning. You've taken an essential step in addressing one of the most vital aspects of life creating a confident relationship with money, both for yourself and your Teen. Together you've explored the importance of breaking down taboos, nurturing open conversations and building practical money habits, that will serve as tools for lifelong financial competence and money confidence.

The journey to financial empowerment is not about having all the answers, it's about asking the right questions, staying curious and embracing the learning process. By opening these conversations and committing to building these skills together, you're creating a legacy that extends beyond numbers. You're cultivating trust, confidence and a sense of responsibility which will ripple through generations.

Your call to action

Now it's time to act; knowledge is only power when it's applied, so here's your challenge:

1. **Start or continue the conversation today** - Reflect on one money lesson you wish you'd been taught as a teen and share it with somebody else, not just your Teen this time. Ask them about their own beliefs, goals, or questions about money.
2. **Commit to one exercise from this book** - If you have not yet taken the time to work through each of the exercises in the book, now is the time to do it! Whether it's creating a budget together with your Teen, setting financial goals, or exploring your money stories, take the first step now.
3. **Be a role model** – Demonstrate to your Teen that learning about money is an ongoing journey. Share your progress, admit your mistakes and celebrate successes, both theirs and yours.
4. **Expand your impact** - Share what you have learnt with other parents and encourage them to

start money conversations with their children. By doing so, you will help build a generation of financially confident and empowered individuals.

5. **Celebrate how far you have come** - Don't forget the importance are celebrating this journey you are now on and marking every milestone - big or small - as a celebration of making the decisions that you have made for you, your Teen and those around you.

As you continue this journey, remember, Money Confidence is the gift that keeps on giving. You are not just teaching your Teen about money, you're equipping them with the tools to navigate life with confidence, resilience and independence.

So, take that first step and keep walking forward, together. I'm proud of you, I hope you are proud of you too. And finally remember Where Mindset Goes Money Grows ®

ADDITIONAL RESOURCES

In Chapter One, you were invited to understand your money story and to answer 10 key questions to help you uncover that story. If you want to take your investigation further, here are an additional 10 questions.

1. What do I think will happen if I become wealthy?

In the book *The Big Leap* by Gay Hendricks, the author talks about how 60% of Lottery winners in the US end up either exactly back where they were financially, or even worse off. How would you feel if you were one of the Lottery winners? Would you fear judgement, too much responsibility, or are you afraid that wealth will change you? These fears can prevent you from creating the habits and behaviours from fully going after financial success.

2. What role does money play in your relationships?

Think about the role money plays in your personal relationships. Is it a cause of resentment, do you avoid talking about it with your family, is it a source of arguments, or celebration? Understanding your relationship dynamics around money can shift and improve communication and reduce conflict and misunderstanding.

3. Am I afraid of money?

Such a simple question, but it can uncover so much. Think about if you have a tendency towards hoarding money, as a result of a fear about losing it or not having enough, even when it might be necessary for you to spend it or invest it. This can be an indication of a scarcity mindset and a lack of trust in your own ability, to make good decisions to generate more income.

4. What is my attitude to debt?

Do you believe that debt is something to be avoided at all costs, or do you see it as a tool that can help you make more money? This question helps to establish whether you have a healthy or unhealthy relationship with money as debt, when managed well, can be an effective tool for wealth generation.

5.   Do I make financial decisions based on logic or emotion?

This is your opportunity to reflect on whether your choices around money are driven by impulse, stress, or fear, or if those decisions are well thought out, well-planned and based on your long-term goals. This will help you to recognise and identify if emotional triggers are influencing your current habits with money.

6.   How do I define financial success?

Use this question to reflect on whether financial success is about having security, freedom, status, or giving to others. If you understand your personal definition of success, this will allow you to be more focused on your financial goals and values and more likely to stick to what needs to be done, to achieve that success.

7.   What would I do if money was not an issue?

This is the opportunity to imagine a life where you have absolutely no financial limitations. How would you spend your time, what would you spend your money on, would your life change and if so, how? This question helps to uncover your true values and real desires and to recognise what might be holding you back currently, due to worries around money.

8.   How often do I review my finances?

Do you regularly check your bank account, do you have a budget that you review frequently? What about savings, investments and spending, are you in control of what these look like and whether they working for or against you? A lack of review can indicate a tendency to bury your head in the sand, demonstrate avoidance, or a lack of financial confidence.

9.   Do I focus more on scarcity or abundance?

Are you constantly worried about money and never have enough, or do you feel grateful for what you have and what is possible for you? Are you a 'glass is half full or half empty' kind of person? Do you spend a lot of time worrying about things that never actually happen? A scarcity mindset can prevent your financial growth and achieving your full potential, because you block access to the part of you that is able to see opportunities and solutions. Having an abundance mindset, can encourage to see the art of the possible, be excited about your own potential and take positive action to create the successful future you want to create for yourself.

10. Am I clear on my financial goals?

Do you have a clear vision for your financial future? Are your goals SMART (Specific, Measurable, Achievable, Relevant and have a Time limit)? This will indicate whether you're taking charge of your life and financial reality or simply reacting to what is going on around you.

ABOUT THE AUTHOR

Lesley Thomas is the founder of The Money Confidence Academy and the voice behind the acclaimed podcast *Let's Talk Money and More*. As a certified Money and Mindset Coach, Lesley has helped thousands of parents, teens and professionals rewire their relationship with money so they can raise the next generation with confidence, clarity and financial freedom.

A sought-after speaker, mentor and creator of the pioneering *Money@Home*™ and *Money@School*™ programmes, Lesley blends real-world financial guidance with deep emotional intelligence. Her work empowers parents to move beyond silence, shame, or outdated scripts and instead model healthy, honest conversations around money.

Through her own experiences as a business owner and mother of two teenage boys, Lesley knows just how powerful financial role-modelling can be and how urgently today's families need these conversations.

Her message is simple: When you own your relationship with money, you show your teen how to own theirs. This isn't just about finances, it's about identity, confidence and rewriting the story for the next generation.

Work With Me

If reading this book has sparked something in you, a desire to change how you think, talk, and feel about money then let's keep the conversation going.
Through The Money Confidence Academy, I support parents to shift their money mindset, overcome long-held blocks, and raise empowered teens by becoming confident, clear, and capable in their own money decisions.
Whether you're looking for:
- A practical framework to rebuild self-trust around money
- Coaching to break through old patterns and beliefs
- Support to become a powerful role model at home
- Workshops and programmes for your school or organisation

There's a way we can work together.

This isn't about quick fixes or one-size-fits-all advice.

It's about creating lasting change from the inside out and it starts with you.

Explore my programmes, events, and 1:1 mentoring here:

www.themoneyconfidenceacademy.com

Or come say hello on LinkedIn:

www.linkedin.com/in/lesley-thomas

Listen to my podcast *Let's Talk Money and More!*

Discover the 5 essential money conversations every teen needs:

"Because confidence with money isn't something you're born with, it's something you build, one decision, one conversation at a time."

Lesley

Printed in Dunstable, United Kingdom